Foundations

for Adult Reading 1

MW00683192

Foundations

for Adult Reading 1

GLENCOE

McGraw-Hill

New York, New York
Columbus, Ohio
Mission Hills, California
Peoria, Illinois

Special thanks to William C. Schick

Text Acknowledgments

6–7 Adapted from "Midshipman Nguyen, 100 percent American" from *Chicago Tribune*, July 3, 1989. Copyright © Associated Press Newsfeatures. Reprinted by permission. **12** Rogers Worthington, "Furniture wars in Omaha." *Chicago Tribune*, October 24, 1989. **12** Robert Dorr, "Customers Arrive Before Mrs. B. Opens." The *Omaha World-Herald*, October 1, 1989. **16** "We Real Cool" by Gwendolyn Brooks from *Blacks*. Copyright © 1987 by The David Company. Reprinted by permission of Gwendolyn Brooks Blakely. **17** Excerpt from "We Real Cool" by Gwendolyn Brooks from *Blacks*. Copyright © 1987 by The David Company. Reprinted by permission of Gwendolyn Brooks Blakely. **20** "Lester Rasmussen: Jane's Blue Jeans" from *Alliance, Illinois* by Dave Etter. Copyright © 1983 by Dave Etter. Reprinted by permission of Dave Etter. **22** "Larry Graham: Empty Beer Can" from *Alliance, Illinois* by Dave Etter. Copyright © 1983 by Dave Etter. Reprinted by permission of Dave Etter. **22** "Estelle Etherege: Fifty" from *Cornfields* by Dave Etter. Copyright © 1980 by Dave Etter. Reprinted by permission of Dave Etter. **29–30** Adaptation of translation from "José Venzor—From Sleeping in the Streets to Owning an Art Gallery" by Ricardo Vela from *Más*, Autumn 1989, p. 53. Reprinted by permission of Ricardo Vela. **42** "José Cruz" from *Class Dismissed II* by Mel Glenn. Copyright © 1986 by Mel Glenn. Reprinted by permission of Houghton Mifflin Company. **45–46** Adapted by permission of Random House, Inc. from *The American Medical Association Family Medical Guide*. Copyright © 1982 by Random House, Inc. **57** "Woman Work" by Maya Angelou from *Saturday's Children: Poems of Work*. Copyright © 1982 by Maya Angelou. Reprinted by permission of The Helen Brann Agency, Inc. **70** Excerpt from "Justin Faust" from *Class Dismissed II* by Mel Glenn. Copyright © 1986 by Mel Glenn. Reprinted by permission of Houghton Mifflin Company. **73** "Justin Faust" from *Class Dismissed II* by Mel Glenn. Copyright © 1986 by Mel Glenn. Reprinted by permission of Houghton Mifflin Company. **78** James Coates, "Marines apologize to a secret weapon." *Chicago Tribune*, April 14, 1989. **82** Excerpted from "Teen mom has little room for fun" from "Dear Abby" by Abigail Van Buren from *Chicago Tribune*, April 1, 1989. Copyright © 1989 by Universal Press Syndicate. Reprinted by permission of Abigail Van Buren. **89** "Primer Lesson" from *Slabs of the Sunburnt West* by Carl Sandburg, copyright 1922 by Harcourt Brace Jovanovich, Inc. and renewed 1950 by Carl Sandburg, reprinted by permission of the publisher. **89** "Deceased" from *In Good Time*. Copyright © by Cid Corman. Reprinted by permission of the author. **102** Adaptation from "Dream Machines" by Danilo Alfaro from *Hispanic*, September, 1989. Copyright © 1989 by the Hispanic Publishing Corporation. Reprinted by permission of Hispanic Publishing Corporation. **122** "Summer Grass" from *Good Morning, America* by Carl Sandburg, copyright 1928 by Harcourt Brace Jovanovich, Inc. and renewed 1950 by Carl Sandburg, reprinted by permission of the publisher. **122** Excerpt from "Roofs & Stars" by Cung Tram Tuong in *A Thousand Years of Vietnamese Poetry*. Copyright © 1974 by Asia Society, Inc. Reprinted by permission of the Asia Society, Inc. **122** "A cooling breeze" by Onitsura from *Haiku in English* by Harold G. Henderson. Copyright © 1965 by Japan Society, Inc. Reprinted by permission of Japan Society, Inc. **136** Excerpt from "We Real Cool" by Gwendolyn Brooks from *Blacks*. Copyright © 1987 by The David Company. Reprinted by permission of Gwendolyn Brooks Blakely. **136** Excerpt from "Lester Rasmussen: Jane's Blue Jeans" from *Alliance, Illinois* by Dave Etter. Copyright © 1983 by Dave Etter. Reprinted by permission of Dave Etter. **136** Excerpt from "Larry Graham: Empty Beer Can" from *Alliance, Illinois* by Dave Etter. Copyright © 1983 by Dave Etter. Reprinted by permission of Dave Etter. **136** Excerpt from "Estelle Etherege: Fifty" from *Cornfields* by Dave Etter. Copyright © 1980 by Dave Etter. Reprinted by permission of Dave Etter. **138** Excerpt from "José Cruz" from *Class Dismissed II* by Mel Glenn. Copyright © 1986 by Mel Glenn. Reprinted by permission of Houghton Mifflin Company. **139** Excerpt from "Woman Work" by Maya Angelou from *Saturday's Children: Poems of Work*. Copyright © 1982 by Maya Angelou. Reprinted by permission of The Helen Brann Agency, Inc.

Photo Credits

All photographs not credited are the property of the Glencoe Division of Macmillan/McGraw-Hill School Publishing Company.
3 *top left*, AP/Wide World; *top right*, AP/Wide World; *bottom left*, Henrietta Spearman/*Atlanta Journal and Constitution*; *bottom right*, Ricardo Vela **5** AP/Wide World **11** AP/Wide World **15** Courtesy Harper & Row **16** Peter Menzel/Stock Boston **28** Ricardo Vela **32** Henrietta Spearman/*Atlanta Journal and Constitution* **37** Courtesy *Fort Wayne News-Sentinel* **41** "José Cruz" from *Class Dismissed II* by Mel Glenn. Copyright © 1986 by Mel Glenn. Reprinted by permission of Houghton Mifflin Company. **53** Mark M. Walker/Picture Cube **59** Erica Stone **81** Frank Siteman/Picture Cube **92** Robert Brenner/PhotoEdit **101** © Max Aguilera-Hellwig

ISBN 0-673-24239-0

Imprint 1996
Copyright © 1991 by Glencoe/McGraw-Hill. All rights reserved. Copyright © 1991 Scott, Foresman and Company. All rights reserved. Printed in the United States of America.
Except as permitted under the United States Copyright Act, no part of this publication may be reproduced or distributed in any form or by any means, or stored in a database or retrieval system, without prior written permission of the publisher. Send all inquiries to:
Glencoe/McGraw-Hill, 936 Eastwind Drive, Westerville, Ohio 43081.

4 5 6 7 8 9 10 11 12 13 14 15   COU-K 03 02 01 00 99 98 97 96

Authors

Sharon Fear

Mary K. Hawley

Luz Nuncio Schick

Consulting Editor

John Strucker
Adult Basic Education Teacher
Community Learning Center
Cambridge, Massachusetts

Foundations Consultants

Don Brunn
Instructor
Downtown Community College Center
San Francisco, California

Geneva Burden
Executive Director
Georgia Literacy Coalition, Inc.
Atlanta, Georgia

Charmaine M. Carney
Instructor/Coordinator
Independent Learning Center
Hawkeye Institute of Technology
Waterloo, Iowa

Mary S. Charuhas
Associate Dean of Adult Continuing Education
    and Extension Services
College of Lake County
Grayslake, Illinois

Kathy Cooper
Training Coordinator
Washington Literacy
Seattle, Washington

Betty Gottfried
Teacher/Teacher Trainer
Adult Basic Education Agency Services
New York, New York

Leann Howard
Adult Basic Education/English as a Second
    Language Resource Instructor
San Diego Community Colleges
Continuing Education Centers
San Diego, California

Shirley Huey
Program Director
Literacy Volunteers of Orange County Schools/
Literacy Volunteers of America in Central
    Florida
Orlando, Florida

Valerie Meyer, Ph.D.
Associate Professor
Department of Curriculum and Instruction
Southern Illinois University at Edwardsville
Edwardsville, Illinois

Jill Plaza
Director
Reading and Educational Consultants
Palatine, Illinois

John H. Redd, Ed.D.
Retired Director of Adult Basic Education
Dallas Independent School District
Dallas, Texas

Gail Rice
Adult Basic Education Teacher
Palos Heights, Illinois

Kathy Roskos
Assistant Professor
Department of Education
John Carroll University
University Heights, Ohio

Contents

Unit 3   Messages   69

Unit 4   Cultures   99

How to Use This Book

Foundations for Adult Reading 1 is a book to help you read. It tells what to *do* as you read. You will use what you know as you read. You will learn to look ahead. You will learn to make good guesses. You will learn how to read new words.

The stories, poems, and articles are for you. Every person reading this book is different. So we picked many different stories. We want you to enjoy what you read.

Each reading has these four parts:

Before You Read

Here you will start thinking about the story. You will do things you should do every time you read. You will also look at words that are important to the story.

 They are marked with a "word bank." You can use these words to make a word bank. You will learn how to make a word bank in Unit 1.

The Reading

This book has many readings. Some are fun or helpful. Some make you think.

In Unit 1, "People," you will read about some surprising people. Unit 2, "Coping," is about how people cope with problems. In Unit 3, "Messages," you will hear from people with a message. And in Unit 4, "Cultures," you will learn about different cultures.

At the end of the book is a longer story. There are no questions with it. It is for you to enjoy and think about. That's what reading is about—learning and having fun.

Questions

After each reading are questions. The answers are in the back of the book.

 Some questions have a picture of a speaking person next to them. These are questions to talk about.

Other questions have lines to write on. Write as much as you can. Don't worry much about spelling. Just get your ideas down. If you can't write all your ideas, tell them to another person. That person can write them for you.

Think About It

This part asks what *you* think. It often asks you to write about your ideas first. Then it may ask you to talk about them with other people. Other people may have a different point of view. You learn more about what you think by talking with other people.

We hope you like your book. Happy reading!

1 People

People are very different. They live in different countries. They eat different foods. They have different ideas. But one thing is the same. All people have stories to tell. In Unit 1, you will read some of their stories.

Thinking About *Why* You Read

Why do people read the paper? They read to find out the news. They read to learn about sports teams. They read for fun.

We read for lots of reasons. You need to know why you are reading. Before you read something, decide why you are reading it.

Look at the next story. What is it called? Look at the picture. Read the first paragraph on page 6. Who is this story about?

Now think about why you will read this story. What do you want to know about Thaison Nguyen? What can the story tell you?

Here is one thing you could ask. Did someone give Thaison Nguyen a chance? What do *you* want to ask about the story? Write it here.

Hints for Good Readers

- Before you read something, decide *why* you want to read it.
- Look at the story. Ask: What is this story about? What can the story tell me?
- Read the story to find answers.

People: "Somebody Gave Me a Chance"

Before You Read

A Word to Know

rescued   to be saved

Say It Right

Thaison Nguyen   (ty SOHN noo yehn)

Saigon   (sy GAHN)

Somebody Gave Me a Chance

His country was at war. Most days American airplanes roared over his Saigon home. Thaison Nguyen was just a boy. He dreamed. He dreamed of flying such airplanes.

In 1975, Vietnam fell to the Communists. Nguyen's father was put in a camp. He didn't come home until 1982.

Thaison and his father and brother tried to get out of Vietnam. Several times they tried to leave by boat. Each time, Communist ships turned them back. Then, in September, 1983, with 35 others, they got away in a fishing boat. Five days later a ship picked them up. It was an American navy ship.

The Nguyens came to Atlanta, Georgia. Thaison changed his name to Eugene. He started school. He learned English. In high school, he did well. He worked on the school paper. He made the soccer team. In 1989, he graduated fourth in his class of 350.

Still he wanted to fly. But not in the air force. "The navy rescued me." If not for the navy, he said, "I would probably be dead."

Nguyen tried to get into the Naval Academy. But there were problems. He did poorly on one test. And there was his size. He was too short, the navy said.

Nguyen didn't give up. He asked Georgia's senators Sam Nunn and Wyche Fowler for help. Fowler's people met with him. He was scared. "I wouldn't get another chance," he said.

He talked of his past. He told them of his dreams. "The story that he told, it moved us," said one. They asked the Academy to take him.

In June, 1989, Eugene Nguyen became a U.S. citizen. In July, he entered the Academy. After the Academy he must spend five years in the navy. Nguyen plans to stay longer. Why? He put it this way: "Somebody picked me out of the ocean, got me here, educated me, and gave me a chance. This is my country."

Questions

1. Look at the question you asked about the story. Was it answered? _____ If so, write the answer. If not, write something else you learned from the story.

   _____

   _____

2. Fill in the missing words. Use words from the box.

airplanes	fly	join
country	leave	navy

Thaison Nguyen lived in Vietnam during the war. He saw many American _____. He wanted to _____ an airplane. After the war, Nguyen's family tried to _____ Vietnam. They left on a boat. The American _____ picked them up. The Nguyens came to America. Thaison went to school. He wanted to _____ the navy and learn to fly. It wasn't easy. But Nguyen is at the Naval Academy now. He says the United States is his _____ .

3. Why did Nguyen want to fly in the navy?
   a. because he did not like the air force
   b. because the navy saved him
   c. because the navy had asked him to join

4. Why did the senators help Nguyen?

   _____

   _____

5. How do you think Nguyen feels about the United States? Explain.

   _____

   _____

Think About It

The navy saved Eugene Nguyen and his family. The navy gave him a chance. Has someone given you a chance? Have you given someone else a chance? Tell a friend about it.

8

Making a Word Bank

How do you remember new words? Here is one way that works. Make a **word bank.**

When you find a new word, write the word on a card. Writing a word helps you keep it in your mind. On the back of the card, write a sentence using the word. This will help you remember what the word means. Keep the cards in a small box. Go over them often.

Sort the cards into groups that go together. Deciding what group to put each word in helps you remember it. Here's an example. Look at these words.

| husband | truck | car | child | taxi |
| bus | wife | daughter | son | train |

Put each word into one of the two groups below. After you use a word, draw a line through it.

Travel Words   **Family Words**

_____   _____

_____   _____

_____   _____

_____   _____

You can also sort word bank words based on how the words are spelled and how they sound. For instance, two words in the list above start with *tr.* They are *truck* and *train.* Can you think of any other words that start with *tr?* All these words could go in the same group.

Here's another way to sort words. Are any of the words in the box hard for you to spell? List them here.

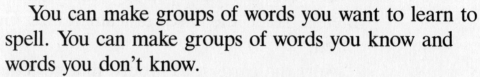

You can make groups of words you want to learn to spell. You can make groups of words you know and words you don't know.

Before each story are a few words to learn. They are called "Words to Know." Add these words to your word bank. Add any other words you read that you want to remember. You can also add words you hear people say. You may want to add words you read in the paper or hear on the radio or TV. Add any word you want to learn to your word bank.

People: "Starting Over—at 95"

Before You Read

WORD BANK

Words to Know

dry goods store   a store that sells cloth, ribbons, and lace

succeed   to do well

Say It Right

Omaha   (OH mah haw)

This story is about a 95-year-old woman. Her life is very busy. Do you want to be busy when you are 95? Write a few words about what you would like.

When I am 95 years old, I want to _____

_____ .

Now read to find out why Rose Blumkin is still busy at age 95.

11

Starting Over—at 95

Mrs. B's Warehouse is doing business. The new lights are not in. It still needs some paint. It's not really open yet. But people are coming in. Perhaps it's because most people in Omaha—and in Nebraska—know Mrs. B.

Mrs. B is Rose Blumkin. This tiny 95-year-old was born in Russia. At 13, she worked in a dry goods store. By 16, she ran the place. At 23, she paid a man some money so she could leave Russia. She came to the U.S. on a peanut boat.

In the 1930s, she and her husband started the Nebraska Furniture Mart. They worked hard. They did well. They made it the biggest family-owned furniture store in the country. In Omaha, it seemed like almost everyone bought furniture from Mrs. B.

The Mart was sold. But Blumkin children continued to run it. Mrs. B went on working there too.

Then came the fight. The family could not agree on how to run the store. Mrs. B walked out. She went home. She tried to take it easy. But she was unhappy. "Go back to work," said her daughters.

So she did. At 95, Mrs. B started over. She already owned a building. It needed work. She found people to do it. She bought furniture to sell. She took on salespeople. Even before she opened, people came to buy.

She has started again. Can she succeed again? Mrs. B is sure she can. "I know how to buy and sell," she says. She also knows how to work. She works each day from nine to five. These days she needs a golf cart to get around. That has not slowed her down. "The day goes too fast," she says.

Questions

1. Fill in the missing words. Use the words in the box.

call	furniture	unhappy
fight	opened	worked

Almost everyone in Omaha knows Rose Blumkin. They _____ her "Mrs. B." For many years, she and her husband sold _____ . Even after their store was sold, the family still _____ there. Then the family had a _____ . Mrs. B left. But she was _____ . She decided to do something about it. At 95, Mrs. B _____ her own store.

2. How do you think Mrs. B felt after her family had the fight? Explain.

_____

_____

3. Do you think Mrs. B will succeed? Explain.

_____

_____

4. Which of these words tell what Mrs. B is like? Circle them. Tell a friend why you think that way.

hardworking	silly	lucky
brave	weak	afraid

Think About It

This is a **time line.** It shows some things in Mrs. B's life. It tells how old she was and what year it was.

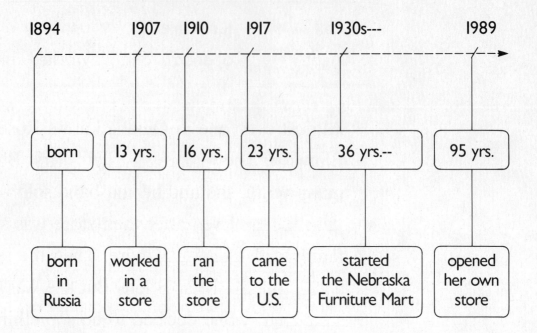

1894	1907	1910	1917	1930s---	1989
born	13 yrs.	16 yrs.	23 yrs.	36 yrs.--	95 yrs.
born in Russia	worked in a store	ran the store	came to the U.S.	started the Nebraska Furniture Mart	opened her own store

 Make your own time line. Show some important things that have happened to you. Share your time line with a friend.

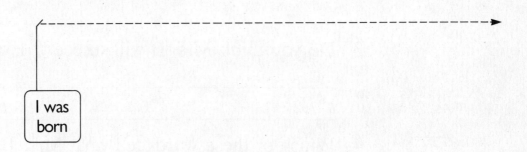

I was born

14

People: "We Real Cool"

Before You Read

A Word to Know

WORD BANK

straight without a curve or bend; in a line

A Reading Tip In the word *straight,* you say the *aigh* like you say *a* in the word *late.*

This next poem is written the way some people talk. You may not understand all the words. But you can understand the message.

Read the poem to yourself. Then read it out loud. Do you like the way it sounds?

About the Poet, Gwendolyn Brooks

Gwendolyn Brooks was born in Kansas in 1917. She moved to Chicago as an infant. She lives there still. She began writing poetry when she was seven years old. In 1950, she won the Pulitzer Prize for her poetry. She was the first black to win a Pulitzer Prize. Since then, she has won many other prizes.

Brooks writes poems about many different things. She often writes about life in black neighborhoods. She talks about the problems and the joys of the people who live there.

Gwendolyn Brooks believes in helping other poets. She gives prizes to children who write poems for her. She gives prizes to adult poets too. Brooks is well loved as a poet and as a friend of poets.

We Real Cool by Gwendolyn Brooks

The Pool Players
Seven at the Golden Shovel

We real cool. We
Left school. We

Lurk late. We
Strike straight. We

Sing sin. We
Thin gin. We

Jazz June. We
Die soon.

16

Questions

1. What word is used over and over in the poem?

   _____

2. Who is speaking in the poem?
   a. some students
   b. some movie stars
   c. some pool players

3. The poem says, "We real cool." What is another way to say the same thing?

   _____

   _____

4. Write *yes* or *no* next to each sentence.

   _____ a. The people in the poem go to school.
   _____ b. The people in the poem stay out late.
   _____ c. The people in the poem sing.

5. Often poems use words that sound the same. In this poem, *cool* and *school* have the same *oo* sound. What other words in the poem have that same sound?

   _____

   _____

6. What other words have that same *oo* sound? Write down any words you can think of.

   _____

   _____

Think About It

The people in the poem say, "We die soon." Why will they die? Write down your ideas.

_____

_____

_____

Picturing What You Read

Good readers make a "picture" of what they read. They look for words that help them feel "right there" when they read. They turn on the TV set in their minds.

Read the next three poems. Try to picture them in your mind. Think about what the people would see. Think about what they would look like. The questions on the side will help you.

Hints for Good Readers

- When you read, try to picture what is happening.
- Look for words that tell what you would see.
- The more you can picture what you read, the better you will understand it.

18

People: Three Poems from Alliance, Illinois

Before You Read

A Word to Know

clothesline   a rope where wet clothes are hung to dry

A Reading Tip   When you see a long word, find the smaller words in it. *Clothesline* is a long word. But there are two small words in it. It is called a *compound word*. What two words do you see in *clothesline?*

You may know someone who makes up stories. Dave Etter made up a whole town! He called the town Alliance. Then he wrote poems about it.

He made up names for all the people in Alliance. He pictured what life was like for each person. In his poems, these people talk about their lives.

Here, three of the people of Alliance speak.

LESTER RASMUSSEN: Jane's Blue Jeans

What would a blue rain look like?

Can you picture these blue jeans?

Hanging alone on a blue-rain clothesline,
hanging alone in a blue rain,
hanging alone:

a pair of torn blue jeans,
a pair of faded blue jeans,
a pair of Jane's blue jeans.

Blue jeans in the shape of Jane,
Jane now in another pair of blue jeans,
blue jeans that also take the shape of Jane.

Oh, Jane, my rainy blues blue-jeans girl,
blue jeans without you inside
is the saddest blue I've seen all day.

Questions

1. What sad thing does Lester Rasmussen see?
   a. Jane's blue jeans
   b. Jane
   c. a rainy day

2. What are Jane's blue jeans like? Tell about them.

   _____

   _____

3. Which of these do you know is true about Jane?
   a. She has died.
   b. She does not love Lester.
   c. She is wearing another pair of blue jeans.

4. Why do Jane's blue jeans make Lester sad?

20

Think About It

Poems are pictures made with words. A poem can be long or short. It can be about a very simple thing, like a pair of blue jeans.

Think of something you see every day. It could be your clock, the dog next door, or a shoe. It can be anything you want. Write a poem about it. It can be short or long. It does not have to rhyme. Share your poem with someone.

Before You Read

Words to Know

WORD BANK

pickup   a small truck with an open back

sags   sinks down

Look at the next two poems. Who speaks in each poem?

_____ and _____

LARRY GRAHAM: Empty Beer Can

Can you picture the beer can being thrown?

What would this sound like?

You write from Pittsfield
that you don't love me anymore.
Once when we were driving around
under a big Pike County moon
you threw a beer can
out the window of my pickup.
Tonight, 200 miles away,
it comes bouncing, end over end,
up to my front door.

ESTELLE ETHEREGE: Fifty

Can you picture the house?

Today, I am fifty years old.

Coming up the hill from the post office,
I can see that my house is in sad shape.
The front porch sags, a window is broken,
and the wind chips off flakes of paint:

51, 52, 53, 54, 55, 56, 57 . . .

Questions

1. In the first poem, who is Larry Graham probably talking to?
   a. his girlfriend
   b. his boss
   c. his sister

2. How do you know?

   _____

   _____

3. What happened when they were driving around in the pickup?
   a. She said she did not love him.
   b. She threw a beer can.
   c. A beer can came to his front door.

4. How are Larry Graham and the beer can alike?

5. In the second poem, what day is it?
   a. Estelle's last day at work
   b. the day Estelle is moving
   c. Estelle's birthday

6. What does Estelle's house look like?

   _____

   _____

7. At the end of "Fifty," what is *really* being counted?
   a. the steps on Estelle's front porch
   b. the flakes of paint
   c. the years that will pass in Estelle's life

8. Do you think Estelle is happy about her birthday? Explain.

   _____

   _____

23

Think About It

Dave Etter wrote all three of these poems. He pretended to be three different people. He tried to picture what they would see and feel.

See if you can write a poem about a person.

- Pretend you are someone else.

- Make up a name.

- Picture what that person is like.

- Write a poem as if you were that person. Write your poem on another piece of paper.

 - Share it with someone else.

People: "Out on a Limb"

Before You Read

A Word to Know

because   for the reason that

When you see this word, stop and pay attention! You're going to learn a reason for something.

This story is about some people who work in a factory. What do you know about factory work? Write your ideas on this *word map*. A word map is a way to order your ideas. Add as many ideas as you can think of. You can draw more circles if you want.

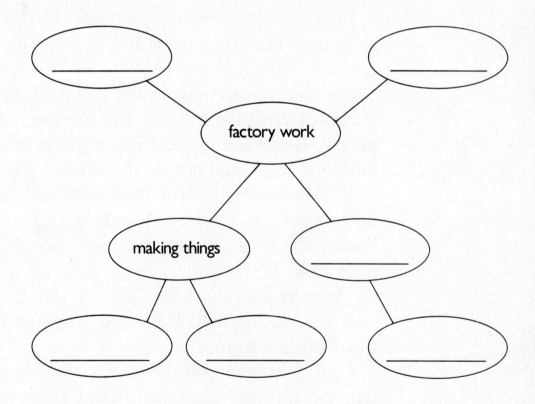

25

Out on a Limb

One time I did the right thing. I'm not brave, believe me. But one time I went out on a limb. It was for a person I didn't even know. And I got cut down.

I worked in a factory. A machine put beans in cans. I made sure the cans were full. It was not a fun job. I did the same thing over and over. But I needed the money. So I was in bad shape when I got fired. It happened because I spoke up for another woman.

Betty was not smart. She was a little strange. She dressed like an old farmer. But she was smart enough to hold this job. She could do it if she worked very hard. It was a big deal for her. She showed up proud and happy the first day. Soon she could do almost any job there.

Like I said, she was very strange. People stayed away from her. They made fun of her. The boss saw this and decided to fire her.

His plan was to make Betty look bad. So the boss made her drive the forklift. The job was hard for most people. It was sad to see Betty try. She could do most jobs. She just could not do the hardest job.

It made me angry. The boss was just being mean. So I went up to the boss. I said, "Can't you give her a break? She works harder than most people. Don't you have a heart?"

The next day, I was fired.

It was hard at first. It was like a slap in the face. But I learned from it.

I got a different job. I like this job. My new boss is fair. We all work as a team. Now I know what kind of boss I want to be! This is one setback that pushed me forward. I hope that's what happened to Betty.

Questions

1. To "go out on a limb" means you take a chance.
   How did the speaker take a chance?
   a. She tried to do the hardest job.
   b. She tried to help Betty.
   c. She went back to school.

2. What was Betty like?

   _____

   _____

3. Why did people stay away from Betty?

   _____

   _____

4. Why did the boss want to fire Betty?
   a. because Betty was lazy
   b. because Betty was very pretty
   c. because the others did not like Betty

5. Why did the boss fire the speaker?

   _____

   _____

Think About It

Have you ever gone out on a limb for someone? What happened?

_____

_____

_____

27

People: "José Venzor"

Before You Read

WORD BANK

Words to Know

pizzeria   a restaurant that serves pizza

art gallery   a place that shows works of art and
sells them

Say It Right

José Venzor   (hoh SAY vehn SOHR)

Look at the name of this story. Look at the picture.
Write one question you think the story could answer.

_____

28

José Venzor: From Sleeping in the Streets to Owning an Art Gallery

He owns the world's largest pizzeria. He owns a gallery of Latin American art in Chicago. José Venzor, from Chihuahua, Mexico, is 42.

José's father died when José was five. His mother found work in El Paso, Texas. José stayed in Mexico. He grew up in homes for children without parents.

These homes made him strong, Venzor believes. They also began his love for art. The children went to church. There, José loved to look at the pictures.

At 15, Venzor lived in Ciudad Juárez. Across the border, in the U.S., was El Paso. Venzor started school in El Paso. He wanted to learn English. School was free to those who lived in El Paso. José said he did. The school found out he did not, and he had to leave.

José heard about jobs in Wisconsin. He decided to go. That's how he came to the Midwest. He worked from five in the morning until twelve at night. He earned $1.32 an hour. He soon got tired of this and moved to Chicago.

For a while, he lived in the streets. Then he found work. He started school again. Then a letter came from the army. He was sent to Vietnam.

The army trained Venzor as a cook. After the army, he opened a restaurant. It didn't do well. The restaurant closed.

Venzor tried again. He opened a small pizzeria near Chicago. This one made money. Today, he has three pizzerias. Three hundred people work for him.

Another dream has also come true. That is his art gallery. His neighbors think it won't last. Venzor believes it will last as long as his love of art lasts.

José Venzor has done much. But he still has many dreams. He says he has just had a lot of luck.

Questions

1. Look at the question you wrote before reading. Was it answered? _____ If so, write the answer.

_____

_____

2. José Venzor started with nothing. Now he has three pizzerias and an art gallery. Show how it happened. Fill in the missing words. Use the words in the box.

art gallery	cook	money
pictures	Wisconsin	

   a. Because he went to church, he learned to love _____ .
   b. Because he wanted a job, he moved to

_____ .
   c. Because he went into the army, he learned to

_____ .
   d. Because he opened a pizzeria, he made lots of _____ .
   e. Because he loves art, he opened an

_____ .

3. Venzor grew up in homes for children without parents. What did the homes do for him? Write *yes* or *no* next to each of these statements.

　　_____ a. The homes made him strong.

　　_____ b. The homes helped him begin to love art.

　　_____ c. The homes trained him as a cook.

4. Venzor says he has just been lucky. Do you think luck was the only thing that helped him? Explain.

_____

_____

Think About It

José Venzor loves art. There are many kinds of art. Drawings, paintings, and photos can be art.

　　Think of a picture that you like. Write a few words about it on the map.

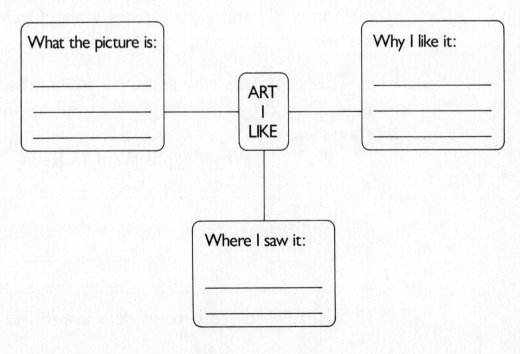

People: "People Learning to Read"

Before You Read

Say It Right

O. D. Guice (gice)

A Reading Tip The three words *could*, *would*, and *should* sound the same. They all end with the same four letters. What are these four letters? _____
Find *could* and *would* in the story. Circle them.

This story tells why some people want to learn to read. Why do you think people want to read? List your ideas.

Why People Want to Read

1. _____

2. _____

3. _____

4. _____

Now read to see if your ideas are in the story.

People Learning to Read

O. D. Guice had a plan. He wanted to own an auto body shop.

He knew he could do it. He had worked in such shops for 20 years. He had learned a lot. He could tell how much a job would cost. He could do a good job on a car.

But Mr. Guice had a problem. He did not read well. He had to read work orders. Sometimes he didn't know what they said.

So, when he was 41 years old, Mr. Guice decided to learn to read. He knew one thing for sure. If he didn't read better, he would never have his own shop.

Mr. Guice went to the Georgia Literacy Coalition. He took classes at least once a week. Sometimes he went two or three times a week.

At GLC, Mr. Guice had many good tutors. The tutors cared about their students. They knew how hard it is for adults to go back to school.

Older people are not like children learning to read. They have many things on their minds. They have jobs. They have families. And they have old or new reading problems to face.

Many people who can't read had a bad time at school. They don't want to go back. They feel sick just thinking about it. Some people who can't read have a problem with letters. They need help to see letters the right way.

People learning to read all want to make a change. They want better jobs. They want to help their children with schoolwork. They want to read letters and bills.

O. D. Guice went to school for three years. He worked hard to read better. Today, he is a busy man.

O. D. Guice now owns Guice Body and Paint Shop in Atlanta. This keeps him busy enough. But once a week, he goes back to school. He teaches other people. He tells them, "You just have to try it. See how it is for you."

O. D. Guice made a change for the better. Now he is helping others do it too.

Questions

1. Look back at your list on page 32. Were some of your ideas about reading in the story? If so, write them here.

   _____

   _____

   _____

2. Why did Mr. Guice want to learn to read?
   a. He wanted to learn about cars.
   b. He did not want to go back to school.
   c. He wanted to have his own shop.

3. Why is learning to read different for adults and children?
   a. Adults need more time for their jobs and their families.
   b. Children have more problems in school.
   c. Adults and children can both have reading problems.

4. What are two reasons some people have problems learning to read?

   _____

   _____

   _____

5. Do you think learning to read helped O. D. Guice? Explain.

_____

_____

_____

Think About It

You are learning to read better. That's why you have this book! What do you want to do when you can read better? Write down your ideas.

When I can read better, I will _____

_____

_____

_____ .

Looking Back

Word Bank

Look over all the words in your word bank. By now you should have ten to fifteen words. What groups can you put them in?

Take out the words that are hard to spell. Copy these words. Then try to write them without looking at the cards. Put aside the words you know.

Make a group of compound words. *Clothesline* and *pickup* would be put in this group.

You can also put all your words in order from A to Z. In this case, *art gallery* might be the first word in your group.

Writing

You have read about many people in this unit. Which person was most interesting to you? Write down his or her name. List some of the things you liked about that person.

What I liked about

_____ :

1. _____

2. _____

3. _____

Now write a few sentences telling what you liked best about that person.

I liked _____ because _____

_____

_____

_____

2 | Coping

Life can be hard. We don't always like what happens to us. We don't always know what to do. Sometimes we want to give up!

But there is hope. We can learn to cope with our problems. In other words, we can learn how to face them. We can do something about them.

In this unit, you will read about ways that people cope with their problems.

Learning New Words

When you read, you see new words. How do you find out what a new word means? Here is one way. Look at the other words around the new word. They may help you understand what it means.

For example, look at the sentences below. Each underlined word is from one of the stories in this unit. Use the other words in the sentences to find out what the new word means.

1. Malcolm was in the hospital for a week. His parents were anxious about his health.
   What could *anxious* mean?
   a. bored
   b. worried
   c. happy

2. If you crouch down behind the chair, no one will see you.
   What could *crouch* mean?
   a. to bite into something
   b. to jump over something
   c. to stoop low or bend over

3. Babies have a lot of curiosity. They are interested in everything around them.
   What could *curiosity* mean?
   a. wanting to know things
   b. getting angry very quickly
   c. having a lot of problems

4. Jeff does <u>data entry</u> at the hospital. He puts the names of all the new patients on the computer.
What could *data entry* mean?
a. being a doctor
b. putting facts into a computer
c. selling computers

5. Sometimes my daughter does something bad. I <u>discipline</u> her by making her stay in her room.
What could *discipline* mean?
a. to train or punish
b. to help
c. to forgive and forget

6. Nathan likes to watch his boss and learn from him. The boss has been a good <u>role model</u> for Nathan.
What could *role model* mean?
a. a person you try to be like
b. an actor who works as a model
c. a new way to make something

7. Ricky has gained <u>weight</u>. All of his clothes are too tight on him now.
What could *weight* mean?
a. how fast something is
b. how heavy something is
c. how tall something is

WORD
BANK

Check your answers. Then add these words to your word bank. Write a new word on one side of a card. Write what the word means on the other side.

Look for new words as you read Unit 2. If you see a new word, stop. Look at the words around it. Look for clues to what the word means. Think about what word makes sense there. Add new words you find to your word bank.

Coping: "José Cruz"

Before You Read

Words to Know

crouch to stoop low or bend down

lbs. short for *pounds*. A pound is a unit of weight.

Look at the name of this poem. Look at the picture. What do you think this poem will be about?

Look at the words in this poem. Some of the words are not spelled correctly. They are spelled the way people *say* them, not the way we *write* them.

Why would the poet do this? He makes us feel like we are really listening to someone talk.

75 lbs.—Get serious.
100 lbs.—A little better.
125 lbs.—Now you're talkin'.
150 lbs.—I can do it.
Whenever I feel the weight of the world
On my shoulders, I go to the gym and work out.
It makes me feel good about myself.
When I crouch to snatch the bar,
I don't think about nothin' else
'Cept puttin' it over my head.
I don't think about
School,
My life,
My future,
Nothin'.
Put on more weights.
I can handle it, man.
No sweat.

Questions

1. What is the speaker talking about in the first four lines?
   a. how much he weighs
   b. how much time he will spend at the gym
   c. how much weight he wants to lift

2. Sometimes the speaker feels "the weight of the world" on his shoulders. What does this mean?
   a. He tries to lift too much.
   b. He feels the weight of all his problems.
   c. He thinks he is too heavy.

3. Why does he go to the gym and work out?

_____

_____

4. What does he think about when he lifts weights?

_____

Think About It

The speaker copes with his problems by going to the gym. What other ways can you cope with your problems? What can you do to forget them for a while? Add your ideas to the map.

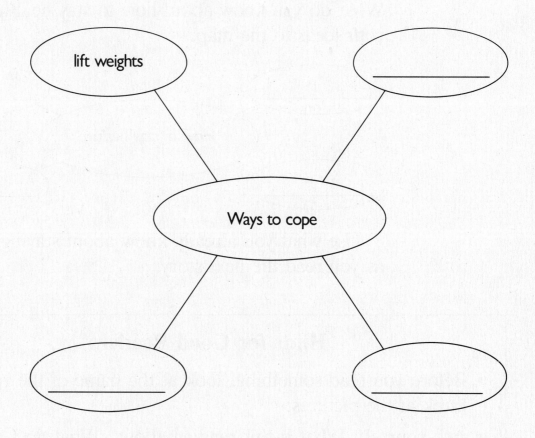

Using What You Know

When you read, you learn new things. But you already know a lot! You can use what you already know to learn more.

When you read about something, think about what you already know about it. For example, imagine you are going to read about job problems. Before you read, think about your own job. Think about the problems *you* have at work. Maybe the reading will talk about some of the same problems. If it does, you already know something about them. Now you can learn more.

The next reading is about how to stay healthy. What do you know about how to stay healthy? Add your ideas to the map.

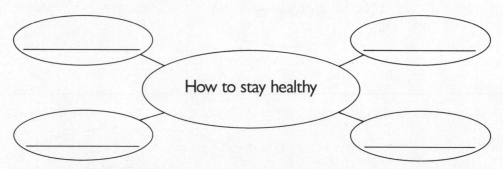

Use what you already know about staying healthy as you read the next story.

Hints for Good Readers

- Before you read something, look at the name of the reading. Look at the pictures.

- Ask yourself: What is this reading about? What do I already know about this?

- *Remember:* Use what you already know to learn more.

Coping: "Five Ways to Stay Healthy"

Before You Read

A Word to Know

WORD BANK

weight   how heavy something is

Five Ways to Stay Healthy

Do you want to feel better? Look better? Live longer? You can, says the American Medical Association. Just follow these rules.

1. Don't smoke. If you do, stop. Now! Smoking can make you sick.

2. Go easy on alcohol. Never have more than two drinks a day.

3. Get some exercise. Exercise hard at least two times a week. Three times a week is better.

4. Eat right. Eat plenty of fruits and vegetables. Cut down on cream, butter, and other high-fat foods. Avoid cake, candy, and other sweets.

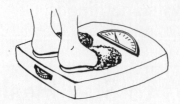

5. Watch your weight. Look at the weight table. Are you too heavy? Then take off some pounds.

A Reading Tip On the next page is a table. It tells how much you should weigh. Here is how to read the table:

The numbers going down the left show how tall a person is. Remember that the marks stand for feet and inches. The first number is 4′10″. This stands for 4 feet 10 inches tall.

The numbers under "Men" and "Women" stand for weight. The first numbers under "Men" are 123–145 lbs. That means 123 pounds to 145 pounds.

Suppose you are a man who is 5 feet 9 inches tall. Go down the left side. Find 5′9″. Then move your finger across the table. Stop under "Men." Your weight should be between 139 pounds and 175 pounds.

If you are this tall—	Your weight should be—	
	Men	*Women*
4'10"	—	100–131 lbs.
4'11"	—	101–134 lbs.
5'0"	—	103–137 lbs.
5'1"	123–145 lbs.	105–140 lbs.
5'2"	125–148 lbs.	108–144 lbs.
5'3"	127–151 lbs.	111–148 lbs.
5'4"	129–155 lbs.	114–152 lbs.
5'5"	131–159 lbs.	117–156 lbs.
5'6"	133–163 lbs.	120–160 lbs.
5'7"	135–167 lbs.	123–164 lbs.
5'8"	137–171 lbs.	126–167 lbs.
5'9"	139–175 lbs.	129–170 lbs.
5'10"	141–179 lbs.	132–173 lbs.
5'11"	144–183 lbs.	135–176 lbs.
6'0"	147–187 lbs.	—
6'1"	150–192 lbs.	—
6'2"	153–197 lbs.	—
6'3"	157–202 lbs.	—
6'4"	—	—

Questions

1. How often should you exercise?

   _____

2. Why shouldn't you eat much cake, candy, and other sweets?

   _____

   _____

3. Suppose you are a man who is 5'6" tall. You weigh 166 pounds. Are you too heavy?

   _____

4. How much should a woman who is 5'3" tall weigh?
   a. between 127 and 151 pounds
   b. between 108 and 144 pounds
   c. between 111 and 148 pounds

Think About It

What is one thing you do now that is *good* for your health?

_____

What is one thing you do now that is *bad* for your health?

_____

What is one *new* thing you would like to do to stay healthy?

_____

Thinking Ahead

Look at this cartoon. What do you think will happen next? Can you make a good guess? Draw a picture showing what you think will happen.

Good readers always think about what could happen next in a story. Before they read, they guess what the story is about. As they read, they make more guesses. They use the information in the story to think about what could happen next.

Hints for Good Readers

- As you read, make good guesses about what could happen next.

- Then read to find out if you were right.

Coping: "When Someone Is Choking"

Before You Read

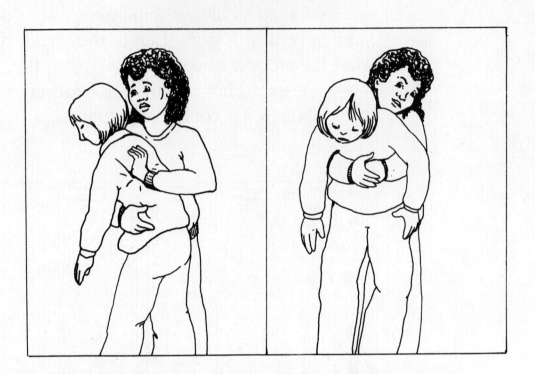

Look at the name of the next reading. Look at the pictures. What do you think this reading is about?

I think this reading is about _____

_____.

Now read to see if you are right. If you are not right, don't worry. It is not important. What is important is to *think* ahead of time about what you read.

When Someone Is Choking

Someone is choking, perhaps on food. The food won't go down. It won't come up either. The person can't get a breath. He or she may even turn blue. People can die from choking. But you can help. Here is what to do:

1. Get behind the person. Put one arm around him or her. Hold tight. With your other hand, give four hard blows high on the person's back. Use the bottom of your hand.

2. If this does not work, stand behind the person. Make a fist with one hand. Put your fist just above his or her waist. Put your other hand over your fist. Pull in and up. Pull hard.

3. If this does not work, do it three more times. If this does not work, give the person four more back blows.

Questions

1. Fill in the missing words. Use the words from the box.

waist	back	hand	behind
blows	pull	fist	times

You can help someone who is choking. First, stand _____ the person. Give four hard blows on the person's _____ . If that does not work, make a _____ with one hand. Put your fist above the other person's _____ .

51

Cover your fist with your other _____ .
Then _____ up and in with your fist. Do
this four _____ . If the person is still
choking, repeat the _____ on the back.

2. What is a sign that someone is choking?
   a. laughing
   b. breathing
   c. turning blue

3. You have learned about a way to help someone
   who is choking. Would you try this if you saw
   someone choking? Explain.

   _____

   _____

Think About It

Sometimes very simple things can save a life. Do you
know a story about someone saving another person's
life? Write a few words about what happened. Then
share the story with someone else.

Who saved the life:	Whose life was saved:
_____	_____

How it was saved:
_____
_____

Coping: "Can Your Child Kick Drugs?"

Before You Read

WORD BANK

A Word to Know

anxious   (ANGK shuhs) worried

This reading is about children who have drug problems. What do you already know about people who are on drugs? Write your ideas on the map.

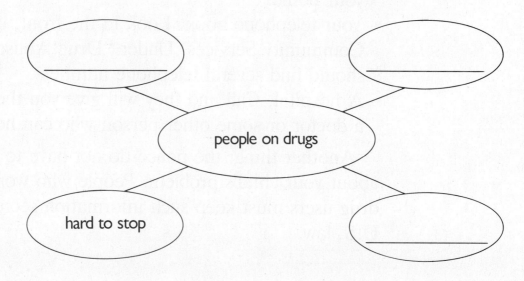

people on drugs

hard to stop

Can Your Child Kick Drugs?

You know your child takes drugs. What can you do? You can talk to your child. You can show your love and support. You can keep the child at home, away from drugs and drug-taking friends. This might work if your son or daughter has only tried drugs a few times.

But what if your child has a habit? Can the child stop on his or her own? The problem may be too much for you and your child to handle alone.

Here is what can happen when a child tries to stop taking drugs:

- The child will be anxious. He or she will want drugs all the time.
- The child's breathing will be quick. He or she may yawn a lot.
- The child may have a runny nose and watery eyes.
- The child may have hot flashes and sweats.
- The child may have chills and get the shakes.

A child with these problems is very sick. This child needs outside help. Here are some places to get that help:

- A telephone hot line. One is 1-800-COCAINE. The person there will tell you where to get help close to your home.
- Your telephone book. Look in the front, under Community Services. Under "Drug Abuse," you should find several telephone numbers.
- A hospital. Call and they will give you the name of a doctor or some other person who can help.

Another thing: the police do not have to know about your child's problem. People who work with drug users must keep such information secret. It is a U.S. law.

Questions

1. What are three things that can happen when a child stops taking drugs?

   _____

   _____

   _____

2. If your child wants drugs all the time, what should you do?
   a. get outside help
   b. let the child take only a few drugs
   c. make your child leave home

3. What are things you can do if your child is on drugs?

   _____

   _____

   _____

4. What are three places where you can look for help?

   _____

   _____

   _____

Think About It

This reading gave some ideas for parents whose children are on drugs. What do *you* think parents should do? Write down your ideas. Share them with someone else.

Parents should _____

   _____

   _____

Coping: "Woman Work"

Before You Read

Poems are written in many different ways. Some poems use words that rhyme. These are words that sound the same in the last part, like *day* and *play*.

Can you think of two other words that rhyme? Write them down.

_____   _____

Read the poem and listen for words that rhyme.

About Maya Angelou

Maya Angelou is a well-known American writer. She is also a singer, a dancer, and an actress. She has visited many parts of the world. She has written poems and plays, and books about her life.

Angelou often writes about the problems of black women in the South. Her own life was not easy. She grew up in a poor part of Arkansas in the 1930s. As a child, she was raped by her mother's boyfriend. At 16, she became a single mother. Some of her books tell about these things. They tell how she worked to become an actress and a writer.

Woman Work by Maya Angelou

I've got the children to tend
The clothes to mend
The floor to mop
The food to shop
Then the chicken to fry
The baby to dry
I got company to feed
The garden to weed
I've got the shirts to press
The tots to dress
The cane to be cut
I gotta clean up this hut
Then see about the sick
And the cotton to pick.

Shine on me, sunshine
Rain on me, rain
Fall softly, dewdrops
And cool my brow again.

Storm, blow me from here
With your fiercest wind
Let me float across the sky
'Til I can rest again.

Fall gently, snowflakes
Cover me with white
Cold icy kisses and
Let me rest tonight.

Sun, rain, curving sky
Mountain, oceans, leaf and stone
Star shine, moon glow
You're all that I can call my own.

Questions

1. Write down some of the words that rhyme in this poem. An example is given.

   <u>   tend   </u>   _____   _____

   <u>   mend   </u>   _____   _____

2. Name three things the woman in the poem has to do.

   _____

   _____

   _____

3. What does she tell the storm to do?
   a. to leave her alone
   b. to blow her to a place where she can rest
   c. to blow away all her problems

4. Why did she call the poem "Woman Work"?

   _____

   _____

   _____

Think About It

How do you think the woman in this poem feels?

She feels _____

_____

Do you ever feel that way? Explain.

_____

_____

_____

Coping: "Some Tips for Parents"

Before You Read

Words to Know

curiosity   wanting to know things

role model   a person you try to be like

discipline   to train or punish

Look ahead at the next reading. What is it about?

_____

Think of a question about the reading. Write it down.

_____

Look for the answer as you read.

Some Tips for Parents

Children are interested in everything. They want to learn. How can a parent help? Here are some ideas.

- **Listen to your child.** Let the telephone ring. Serve dinner late if you have to. Stop and talk to your child. If you don't, the child may give up. Curiosity can be killed.

- **Show your child the world.** Read books. Meet interesting people. Listen to music. Take trips. They don't have to be long trips. Go to museums. Visit the fire station. Teach your child to cook.

- **Don't try to measure your child against others.** All children are different. All are special. Let your child know he or she is special.

- **Don't keep your child too busy.** Let your child lie in bed. Let him or her do nothing. Children need time to dream.

- **Let your child be interested in just one thing.** Does she live for horses? Is that all she reads about? Don't worry. She is learning other things too. She may be learning how to look things up or take notes.

- **Let your child have friends of different ages.** Older friends make role models. Younger friends can teach your child to lead. Remember, always make sure you meet your child's friends.

- **Discipline your child.** Make rules. See that they are followed.

Questions

1. Look at the question you wrote down before reading. Was it answered? If so, write the answer.

   _____

   _____

2. Why is it important to listen to your child?

   _____

   _____

3. Why shouldn't you compare your child to other children?

   _____

   _____

4. Which of these is NOT good for a child?
   a. Let your child be interested in just one thing.
   b. Let your child have friends of different ages.
   c. Keep your child busy all the time.

5. Are there any tips in the reading that you do NOT agree with? If so, tell which ones. Explain.

Think About It

This reading gave some ideas for helping children learn. What are *your* ideas? How can parents help their children learn? Write down your ideas. Then share them with someone else.

My ways to help children learn

   _____

   _____

   _____

Reading in Phrases

A **phrase** is a group of words. The words go together. When we speak, we stop a little between phrases. Listen to a friend talk. Do you hear short stops? These short stops mark the phrases.

Reading one word at a time makes it hard to get meaning. Read the words below to a friend. Stop five seconds after each word. (Use a watch or count to five slowly.)

Anita   made   an   office   at   home.   The   bank   put   a   computer   in   there.

Did you forget what you were reading about? This can happen when you read too slowly.

The words in a phrase make meaning together. So it makes sense to read them together. Read this:

Anita made an office   at home.

The bank   put a computer   in there.

Here are some sentences from the story "Do Your Homework!" Put a line after the phrases in these sentences. The first one is done for you.

1. How can I go / to work? /

2. I'll need money for child care.

3. And I need new clothes.

4. I haven't worked in years.

Commas, dashes, and periods help you make breaks. Try reading the sentences below. Draw a line after each phrase. The first is done for you.

5. Anita made an office / at home. The bank put a computer in there. They put in a telephone line. She started working the next day.

Something to Think About

Look back at the poems on pages 42 and 57. Often poets like to write one or two phrases on a line. Why do you think they do that?

Try reading the next story in phrases. Read the story silently. Then read it aloud. Listen for the stops. Then read it again silently. The first paragraph has spaces between the phrases. In the rest of the story, draw a line after each phrase.

A Reading Tip   Move your eyes over each whole phrase. Stop at the end of the phrase.

Hints for Good Readers

- Read a phrase at a time. Stop between phrases.
- Look for commas, dashes, and periods. They help you know where to stop.

Coping: "Do Your Homework!"

Before You Read

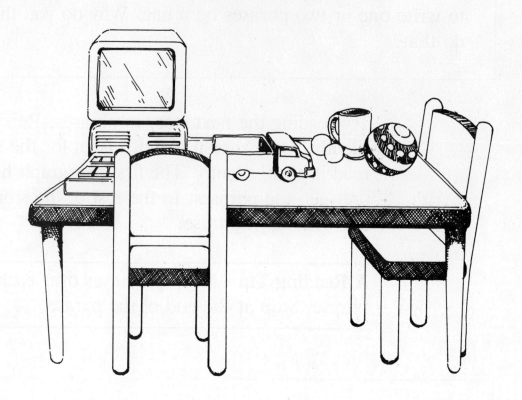

WORD BANK

A Word to Know

data entry   putting facts into a computer

More and more people work at home. The next story talks about Anita, who works at home on a computer. Would you like to work at home? Why or why not?

_____

_____

Now read to see if Anita likes her job at home. Remember to draw a line after each phrase.

Do Your Homework!

Anita was so proud. She had done it. She had passed the final. She had finished near the top of her class. Now she could find a job.

Anita was ready to be a data entry clerk. But something was wrong. She told me about it.

"How can I go to work? I'll need money for child care. And I need new clothes. I haven't worked in years. All my clothes are old," she said.

"And don't forget about bus money, Anita," I said. She just shook her head.

But I had an idea. "I know this bank. They let people work at home," I told her. "You should talk to them."

She did. And she got the job. The bank put a computer in her home. They put in a telephone line too. She started working the next day.

I saw her a few weeks later. "How is the job going?" I asked.

"It's great," she said. "They don't care when I do my work. I just have to get it done. Now I can be with my little girl."

I asked her, "When do you find the time to work? A child takes up so much time."

Anita smiled. "I have to be smart. I get up around six. I make coffee. I work two hours. Then Linda wakes up.

"We have breakfast. After breakfast, Linda plays in the office. I work as much as I can. I have to stop all the time. I have to watch her. But I get an hour or two in before lunch."

"What about the afternoon?" I asked.

"Even better," she said. "Linda sleeps for an hour. I get more done than in the morning. By dinner, I have six hours of work in. I do the last two hours after Linda goes to bed."

I could see Anita was very happy. She loved her job.

Questions

1. Why was Anita worried about getting a job?
   a. She didn't want to work.
   b. She didn't know what kind of work to do.
   c. She didn't have money for child care or clothes.

2. What did the bank do so Anita could work at home?

   _____

   _____

3. Write 1, 2, 3, and 4 to show the order that things happen in Anita's day.

   _____ a. Linda takes a nap and Anita works.

   _____ b. Linda plays in the office while Anita works.

   _____ c. Anita puts Linda to bed and works her last two hours.

   _____ d. Anita gets up, makes coffee, and works for two hours.

4. Why does Anita like working at home?

   _____

   _____

Think About It

 You have read about Anita's job. *Now* what do you think about working at home? What is good about it? What is bad about it? Share your ideas with someone else.

What I would like about working at home:

_____

_____

What I would *not* like about working at home:

_____

_____

Looking Back

WORD
BANK

Word Bank

Look over the words in your word bank. Do you remember what each one means? Choose three words from your word bank. Write sentences using these words. Have someone else read your sentences. Talk about the meanings of the words. Can he or she tell the meanings of the new words?

Writing

In this unit you read about people's problems. You read about how people cope with problems. You learned some things you can do to cope.

Think of a problem you had. It can be a big one or a small one. Write a letter to a friend. Tell the friend about your problem. Tell what you did about it. Tell your friend how you feel about it now.

Dear _____ ,

I had a problem. It was that _____

_____

_____

This is what I did about it. _____

_____

_____

Now I feel _____

_____

Your friend,

_____

3 Messages

People send messages all the time. We all have something to say! It may be an important message, maybe one about a birth or a death. It may be an angry message. It may be a happy one.

We have many ways of sending messages. We can talk to someone. We can write a letter. We can even send a message with our eyes!

Using Clues to Read New Words

How can you learn to read a new word?

1. You can use **meaning clues.** Think about the meaning of the words and sentences around the new word.

2. You can use **what-you-know clues.** Use what you already know about life to think about the word.

3. You can use **sound clues** in the new word.

Here are some words you will read in Unit 3. Try using clues to read them.

1. divorce
This word is in a poem in Unit 3.

> I know that a <u>divorce</u> is supposed to be
>   no big deal these days.
> Try telling that to my mother, who
>   still sometimes sets the table for three.
> Try telling that to my father, who
>   calls daily, "to keep in touch," he says.

Look for **meaning clues** in the sentences after the word. Answer this question to find the clues:
The mother and father
  a. live together.
  b. live apart.
Underline the words in the poem that tell you this.

Now use **what you know** about life to answer this question:

What do a mother and father get when they want to live apart?

They get a d_____ .
Therefore, what is divorce?

    a. when a husband and wife split up
    b. when a child leaves home

You can use **sound clues** to say *divorce*. What is the first sound? _____ How do you say the *c*? Like an *s* or like a *k*? Try saying it both ways before you decide.

2. bartender

This word is in a story about a talking dog.

    A man walked into a bar. Behind him was a dog. The man sat down. The dog did too.
    "How's it going?" the <u>bartender</u> asked.

First look for **meaning clues.**
Where are the man and the dog?

_____

Now use **what you know** about life.
Who serves drinks in a bar?

_____

Now look for **sound clues** to say the word.
Bartender is a compound word. What two words are in it?

b_____ t_____

Messages: "Justin Faust"

Before You Read

A Word to Know

divorce   the ending of a marriage

Look at the picture. How do you think the boy is feeling?

In this poem, Justin Faust tells us about his feelings.

Justin Faust by Mel Glenn

I know that a divorce is supposed to be
    no big deal these days.
Try telling that to my mother, who
    still sometimes sets the table for three.
Try telling that to my father, who
    calls daily, "to keep in touch," he says.
My mother's not happy because I'm not happy.
I'm not happy because my mother's not happy.
A circle of pain surrounds empty evenings
And long weekends.
My mother still cries alone at night.
I hear her.
My father fights his tears over the telephone.
I hear him.
I speak to both of them practically every day.
I wish they would speak to each other.

Questions

1. What is Justin Faust sad about?

   _____

   _____

2. The poem says, "A circle of pain surrounds
   empty evenings/ And long weekends." How
   would you say this in your own words?

   _____

   _____

   _____

3. What is one thing the poem says about Justin's father?
   a. Justin's father cries at night.
   b. Justin's father is happier now.
   c. Justin talks to his father on the telephone.

4. What does Justin wish his parents would do?

   _____

   _____

Think About It

 Divorce is very hard for a man and a woman. It is also hard for their children. What do you think parents can do to help their children deal with divorce? List some of your ideas. Then share them with someone else.

How to Help Children After a Divorce

1. _____
2. _____
3. _____
4. _____

Asking Yourself Questions

Alicia read the sign. She asked herself a question about it. She found out the answer. And she was glad she did!

Good readers ask questions about what they read. Then they read to find the answers. The answers help them understand more about the reading.

Before you read, think ahead about the story. Here are some things you can ask:

- Who is this reading about?

- What is this reading about?

As you read, look for the answers. Then find out more about the reading. Ask:

- What is happening?

- Why does it happen?

- What will happen next?

Sometimes you may not find all the answers. Then you can ask:

- Do I need to know these answers to understand the story?

- Can I find the answers if I look at the reading again?

- Where else could I look for answers?

As you read the next story, think of some things to ask about it. Some examples will be given.

Hints for Good Readers

- Before you read, think of some things to ask about the story.

- As you read, look for the answers. Then ask yourself more about the reading.

- After you read, think about what you asked about the reading. Did you find all the answers? Do you need the answers? Where else could you look for them?

Messages: "Navajo Code-Talkers"

Before You Read

Words to Know

code   a secret way of writing or sending messages

insulting   being rude or mean to someone

Say It Right

Navajo   (NAH vah hoh)

Athapaskan   (ath uh PAS kuhn)

Look at the name of this reading. Look at the picture. Can you guess what the reading is about? Write down your ideas.

_____

_____

Now write down a question you want to ask about the story.

_____

_____

Look for the answer as you read.

WORD BANK

Navajo Code-Talkers

World War II. The Pacific. The U.S. is fighting Japan. The radio men are on the front lines. They send important messages.

Messages must be secret, of course.

They are in code. The Americans have several codes. The Japanese break them all. Except one.

This code is Athapaskan. It is spoken by the Navajo.

There were 400 Navajo code-talkers. All were marines. They were trained in radio and sent to the front. There they sent messages in Athapaskan.

But it was more than that. They spoke another code in Athapaskan. It was a code inside a code. Even another Navajo could not understand it.

The code was top secret until 1968. The Navajo were ordered to tell no one. They were men of honor. They kept their secret for 20 years. So no one knew of these brave men.

Now their story is being told. In 1989, Marine General A. M. Gray spoke in Phoenix, Arizona. During the war, a lot of soldiers treated the Navajo badly. He said, "We called them 'Geronimo' and 'Chief.' It was insulting."

He had come to say "we are sorry." And, after all this time, "thank you."

About 250 code-talkers are still living. About forty heard the general speak.

Questions

1. Look at the question you wrote down. Was it answered? If so, write the answer.

   _____

   _____

2. Why would the messages sent during a war have to be secret?

   _____

   _____

3. What is Athapaskan?
   a. a language spoken by the Navajo
   b. a Navajo radio man
   c. a town in Japan

4. Why couldn't the Japanese break the Athapaskan code?
   a. It was top secret.
   b. It was a code inside a code.
   c. The Japanese didn't have radios.

5. Why didn't people know what the Navajo radio men did?
   a. The radio men were too far away from the U.S.
   b. People did not believe the Navajo could do it.
   c. It was a secret for many years.

6. Why did General Gray say "we are sorry" to the Navajo code-talkers?

   _____

   _____

Think About It

There are many ways to make a code. One way is to let a number stand for each letter. Here is a simple code. When you figure it out, you will have a better idea of what a code is.

The Code

A	B	C	D	E	F	G	H	I	J	K	L	M
1	2	3	4	5	6	7	8	9	10	11	12	13

N	O	P	Q	R	S	T	U	V	W	X	Y	Z
14	15	16	17	18	19	20	21	22	23	24	25	26

A Message in Code

Try to read this message. It is written in the code above.

23-5   23-9-12-12   19-20-18-9-11-5
1-20   13-9-4-14-9-7-8-20.
20-5-12-12   14-15   15-14-5!

This code is easy to break. The Navajo code was much more difficult. But it was based on the same idea. Why do you think the Japanese could never break the Navajo code?

_____

_____

Messages: "Dear Abby, I'm a 16-Year-Old Single Mom"

Before You Read

For many years, people have written to Abigail Van Buren, or "Dear Abby." They write her letters about their problems. The letters and her answers are printed in the paper every day.

The next reading is about a letter written to "Dear Abby." Look at the name of the reading. What do you think the letter will be about?

Now read to see if you are right.

That's how the letter begins. Her son is three months old. She works. She goes to school. She wants other teens to know it's hard. This is her day:

5:00 a.m.: wake up.
5:15 a.m.: take shower and get ready for school.
6:00 a.m.: wake up and dress my son.
6:15 a.m.: take my son to day-care.
6:30 a.m.: go to school.
1:30 p.m.: pick up my son at day-care.
2:00 p.m.: give my son a bath.
2:30 p.m.: feed him.
3:00 p.m.: unpack his diaper bag and repack a new one.
3:30 p.m.: play with my son.
4:00 p.m.: get ready for work.
5:00 p.m.: go to work.
9:15 p.m.: come home, feed my son, and put him to bed.
9:30 p.m.: make formula for the next day.
10:00 p.m.: clean up the house, do laundry and homework.
11:00 p.m.: go to bed.

She is often up at night with her son.

There is no time for the kind of fun most 16-year-old girls have.

Luckily, she lives at home. Her parents help. But money is a problem. She pays for day-care. That leaves her $80 a month.

She is trying, she says. "It's not easy." Some teens think having a baby is no problem. She wants them to know what it's really like.

Questions

1. Why did "16-Year-Old Single Mom" write her letter?
   a. to ask for money
   b. to tell others that it's hard to be a young, single mother
   c. to tell others they should be young, single mothers too

2. What does she do in the evening?
   a. She goes to school.
   b. She works.
   c. She goes out with friends.

3. How many hours of sleep does she get?

   _____

4. She has $80 a month to spend. What are some of the things she would need to buy? List them.

   _____

   _____

   _____

   _____

   _____

5. Are you as busy as the young mother you have read about? Make a list of the things you do in a day. If you need more room, use a sheet of paper.

   My Day

Think About It

Imagine that you are "Dear Abby." You want to answer the letter from the young mother you just read about. What would you say to her? Write your answer.

DEAR SINGLE MOM,

_____

_____

_____

_____

_____

_____

Messages: "The Dog's Tale"

Before You Read

A Word to Know

WORD BANK

rough   (ruhf) hard

A Reading Tip   The word *rough* is not spelled the way it sounds. The *gh* has an *f* sound.

Here are some other words that are like *rough.*

　　　　　　　　enough　　　tough

Use *rough, tough,* or *enough* in these sentences.

1. We had en_ _ _ _ cake to eat.
2. The dog had a r_ _ _ _ day.
3. The meat was t_ _ _ _ because it was cooked too long.

You know that words can have more than one meaning. Sometimes writers play with different meanings of a word to make a story funny. For example, read the name of this story out loud. What is funny about the word *tale?*

Now read to find other ways the writer plays with words.

The Dog's Tale

A man walked into a bar. Behind him was a dog. The man sat down. The dog did too.

"How's it going?" the bartender asked.

"Fine," said the man.

"Rough," said the dog.

"What you got there?" the bartender asked.

"Him? A talking dog," the man answered.

"Oh really?" the bartender said. He had his doubts.

"Really," the man said. "Talk to him. Give us both a free beer if he talks back."

"Is this a joke? Me talk to a dog?" the bartender said. The dog rolled his eyes.

"Go on. Ask him something. We want our free beer," the man said. The dog pounded on the bar.

"What should I ask? Which stock I should buy?" the bartender asked. The dog looked worried. He knew nothing about the stock market.

"He can't tell the future," the man said. The dog looked happier.

The bartender said, "I don't know what to ask. You ask him something."

The man did. "Sparky, what do you call the outside of a tree?"

"Bark, bark. Bark," the dog answered. He had a low voice. But you could make out the word.

The bartender was angry. "Bark? You call that talking? No beer for you!"

The man said, "You think that was too easy? Go ahead. Ask him something hard."

"Like what?" the bartender said.

"Ask him something about baseball. He loves to talk about baseball," the man said. The dog nodded.

The bartender thought for a moment. "Who was the greatest baseball player of all time?"

The dog felt strongly about this. He got excited. "Ruth, Ruth. Ruth," he kept saying in his low voice. It sounded very much like barking.

"Do you think I'm stupid? This dog can't talk," the bartender roared. He threw the man into the street, and the dog after him.

The dog picked himself up. He dusted himself off. He marched back into the bar. He looked the bartender in the eye and said, "OK. You win. How about Willie Mays?"

Questions

1. What do the man and the dog want the bartender to give them?

   _____

2. In the story, the dog says "rough," "bark," and "Ruth." What do these words sound like?

   _____

3. Why doesn't the bartender think the dog is talking?
   a. He thinks the man is talking for the dog.
   b. When the dog talks, it sounds a lot like barking.
   c. The bartender doesn't hear well.

4. When the dog says, "Ruth, Ruth," who is he talking about? (You have to be a baseball fan to know this answer!)

   _____

5. At the end of the story, what happens?
   a. The dog really talks.
   b. The dog barks.
   c. The bartender laughs at the dog.

Think About It

 There are a lot of jokes about talking animals. Do you know any? Try to remember some animal jokes. Share your jokes with a group of people. Then write down the joke you like best.

_____

_____

_____

_____

Messages: "Primer Lesson" and "Deceased"

Before You Read

A Word to Know

WORD BANK

deceased   (dih SEEST) dead

Even though these poems are short, they say a lot. As you read, think about what the writers want to say about life.

Primer Lesson   by Carl Sandburg

Look out how you use proud words.
When you let proud words go, it is
   not easy to call them back.
They wear long boots, hard boots; they
   walk off proud; they can't hear you
   calling—
Look out how you use proud words.

Deceased   by Cid Corman

it comes back
unopened

why open
to see what I said

there was
much to tell you

now there is nothing
to say

Questions

"Primer Lesson"

1. A primer is a schoolbook for children. Why would the first poem be called "Primer Lesson"?
   a. It teaches something children should learn.
   b. It is an easy poem to understand.
   c. The poem is about what happens in school.

2. What happens when you use proud words?
   a. You get what you want.
   b. You can't take them back.
   c. People like you more.

3. Give an example of someone using proud words.

"Deceased"

4. What comes back unopened?

   _____

5. Why does the letter come back?
   a. It had the wrong address.
   b. The person it was sent to didn't want to open it.
   c. The person it was sent to died.

6. Why is there "nothing to say" now?

   _____

7. How do you think the person in the poem feels when the letter comes back?

   _____

   _____

Think About It

"Deceased" is like a story with some pieces missing. We know someone wrote a letter to another person. We know the other person died. But we don't know anything about the people. Were they brothers? A mother and daughter? Old friends? We don't know. We don't know what the letter said either.

Make up your own pieces for the story. Tell who wrote the letter and who died. Tell what the letter said.

Who wrote the letter:
_____

Who died:
_____

What the letter said:
_____
_____
_____

Messages: "Bad Fight, Good Fight"

Before You Read

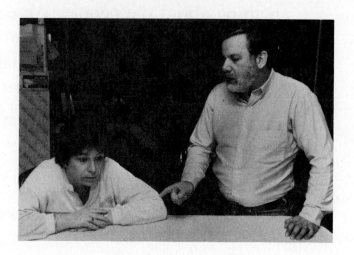

Words to Know

couple   two people

argument   a fight with words

A Reading Tip   Do you have trouble reading long words like *argument?* Break the word into parts. Each part may be easy to read.

You can break *argument* this way:

ar / gu / ment

The first part and the last part are easy to say. The middle part, *gu,* is harder.

This reading is about a couple that argues. Do you think couples should argue? Write a few words about your ideas.

Bad Fight, Good Fight

Dan and Rita had a bad argument. It went something like this.

One night Dan came home late. He had been working hard.

Rita wanted to go out. She had been working hard too. She wanted to have some fun.

"I just want to go to sleep," Dan said.

"But we never go out anymore," Rita said. "You always work late."

"You know I have to work late," he said.

"Well, I work hard too," she said. "And I'm not tired. We never go out anymore!"

"What are you trying to say? Should I quit my job?" Dan asked. He was getting angry.

"No," Rita screamed. "You never listen to me." She started crying.

"Yes I do," he said. "You want to go out? Fine, go out. And I'll go out too. Good-bye!"

Dan left. Rita stayed home crying. When he got back, she was asleep.

The next day, they didn't talk. The day after, they talked about other things. But they didn't talk about the fight. A few days later, it's no surprise. They argued again.

What makes this a bad argument? Dan and Rita blew up at each other. No one won. Dan got no rest. Rita didn't go out.

They wasted a chance to talk. Instead, they hurt each other. It was a bad fight.

But they could have a good fight. This is what they could do.

Rita could tell Dan what she feels. Last time she told him what *he* was doing wrong. She said, "You always work late." Next time she could say, *"I feel* lonely when we don't have time together."

Dan could tell Rita what *he* needs. Last time he said, "Should I quit my job?" He knew Rita didn't want that. Next time he could say, *"I need* more time alone."

Both could stop telling the other person what to do. Instead, they could listen. They could say how they feel.

Then they could find a way to work things out. Maybe Dan can take a nap after work. Maybe they can plan something special on their days off.

A fight can be a good fight. The couple just has to talk and listen. And a good fight can even bring them closer together.

Questions

1. What does Rita want?
   a. to sleep
   b. to go out
   c. to quit her job

2. What does Dan want?
   a. to sleep
   b. to go out
   c. to quit his job

3. What happens in the story?
   a. Dan goes out.
   b. Rita goes out.
   c. Dan and Rita go out.

4. How do Dan and Rita feel after the argument?

_____

_____

5. What is one thing they could do next time they have an argument?

_____

_____

6. The reading says it can be good to fight. Why?

Think About It

What do you think makes a bad fight? What makes a good fight?

Write down what you think happens in a bad fight. Then write down the things that happen in a good fight.

What happens in a bad fight?	What happens in a good fight?
_____	_____
_____	_____
_____	_____

Looking Back

Word Bank

By now your word bank has many words. Many are from stories in this book. Maybe you also have words you heard as you talked with other people. Did you write a sentence using each word? If not, do so now.

Make a group of words that are all alike in some way. Ask someone to guess how the words are alike.

You could also make a group of hard-to-spell words. Many people have trouble spelling *deceased*. Another hard word to spell is *rough*.

Make a group of words that are hard for you to spell. Copy each word several times. Each time you write the word, your spelling gets better.

Writing

In this unit you have read about messages. Think of a message you would like to send. It can be to one person or many people.

You can write to someone who is close to you:

- your husband or wife

- your child

- your parents

- a friend

Or someone you have never met:

- the President of the U.S.

- the mayor of your town

- a TV or movie star

Or many people:

- teenagers
- people who are married
- people learning to read
- teachers

Think about the best way to tell your message. You can write a letter, a poem, or a speech. You can write a song or a story.

Who the message is for:

What the message is about:

_____

_____

Now write your message.

_____

_____

_____

4 | Cultures

People have many different ways of doing things. We have different beliefs. Sometimes we are different because we come from different countries. Sometimes it's because we live in a big city or in a small town. In one country, there are many different cultures.

In this unit, you will read about people in different cultures. As you read, ask: What cultures would I like to know more about?

WORD BANK

Word Bank Puzzle

Look at these word bank words from Unit 4. Fill in the puzzle by matching the words and their meanings.

The first word is done for you.

After you do the puzzle, make a card for each word. Put the cards in your word bank.

Word Bank Words

accent
aches
cattle drives
hitchhiking
outlaws
rodeo
urban

DOWN

1. when cowboys move cattle many miles from their ranches to the markets

2. robbers

3. asking for rides from people passing by on a road

4. from the city

ACROSS

5. a different way of saying words

6. hurts, has pain

7. a contest where cowboys show how well they can rope cows and ride horses

Cultures: "High on Lowriding"

Before You Read

Look at the name of this story. Look at the pictures. Can you guess anything about lowriding? Write down some words about it. Then read to see if you are right.

I think lowriding is _____

_____.

High on Lowriding

They are cars. But such cars!

Take a look at one of them. Rigo Reyes owns a 1959 Chevy Impala. He calls it "Azteca." Outside, the paint is as hard and bright as glass. Lines and circles reach around the sides. Beautiful pictures cover the front end. Special chrome wire wheels shine.

Inside, it's like a living room—or a palace. Rich cloth covers the seats. Seats turn from side to side. The seats go flat and make a bed. Climb in. You can listen to music. You can watch TV. What kind of car is this?

These wonders are called lowriders. So are the men who make them. Lowriders often get together. They drive the streets, showing off their machines. They call it "lowriding."

Lowriding began among Mexican Americans. In the 1930s, young men put rocks in their cars to lower them. Now the cars are lowered with pumps.

What can today's lowriders do? Start one up. Then hold on! It can drop to the ground. It can go up on two wheels. It can jump straight up and go leaping down the street.

Today, lowriders have their own clubs. Some men spend $50,000 on their cars. Fathers pass their cars down to their sons.

What is lowriding? Is it art? Is it sport? Or is it love? Maybe it's all three.

Questions

1. Which of these things could be a lowrider?
   Write *yes* or *no* for each one.

   _____ a. a special kind of car

   _____ b. a man who makes a lowrider

   _____ c. a bicycle

2. What could be another name for this story?
   a. "Lowriders: Dangerous Cars"
   b. "Lowriders: Fancy Cars"
   c. "Lowriders: Cheap Cars"

3. Why do you think the cars are called "lowriders"?

   _____

   _____

4. Do you like the way lowriders look? Tell what you do or don't like about them.

   _____

   _____

Think About It

Read the last paragraph of the reading again. On the map, write your ideas about lowriding. Then see if other people agree with you.

It is like a sport because
_____
_____

It is like art because
_____
_____

Lowriding

It is like love because
_____
_____

103

Finding the Main Idea

Tuesday Night Movies

Mason's Murder Someone is trying to kill Johnny Mason. Will Johnny be able to stop him?
The Dragon's Secret A karate master faces her oldest enemy.

Where Is Mandy? A family searches for their missing child.
Sweet Talk Alex loves Maggie. Is she the only one he loves?

Which movie would you like to see? The paper tells a little about each one. It tells you the **main idea** of each movie.

Try this with a friend. Think of a movie you have seen. See if you can tell your friend the main idea of the movie. Keep it short!

Finding the main idea is important when you read. It will help you in two ways:

1. You will understand what you read.

As you read, ask, "What is this about?" Look for the main idea. If you are not sure, stop and think. Sometimes you may need to go back and read again.

When you finish reading, stop again. Try to say what the story was about in one or two sentences.

2. You will remember what you read.

The main idea is like a coatrack. You can hang **details** of the story on it. Details are the smaller parts of a story. The most important details tell about the main idea.

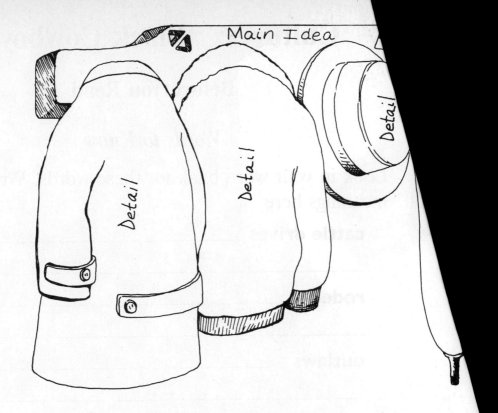

When you hang your things on a coatrack, they ar[e] easier to find. If you "hang" details on the main idea of a story, they will be easier to remember.

Hints for Good Readers

- When you read, ask, "What is this about?" Try to say the main idea in one or two sentences.

- Think of a few important details. Hang them on the main idea. You will remember them better.

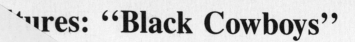

...tures: "Black Cowboys"

Before You Read

Words to Know

...rd bank for these words. Write their

_____

_____

_____

_____

...ws _____

_____

...s reading is about black cowboys in the American
...est. What do you already know about cowboys? Put
some things you know on the map.

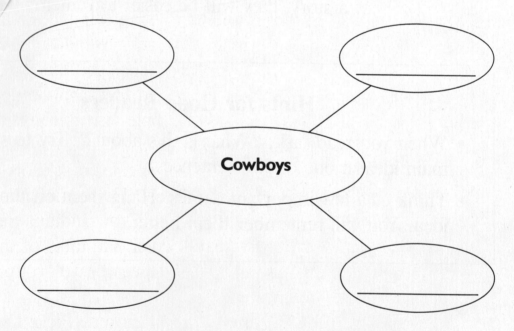

As you read, look for the main idea in each
paragraph. Fill in the missing letters in the notes at
the side.

Black Cowboys

Paul Stewart played cowboys and
I_ _ _ _ _ _.

He met a bl_ _ _
c_ _ _ _ _.

learned about blacks in the American
W_ _ _

runs a
m_ _ _ _ _
in D_ _ _ _r

tells about a black
ch_ _ _ and black
sol_ _ _ _ _

Nat Love, a
gr_ _ _ sh_ _

As a boy, Paul Stewart played
Indians. Paul was always the Ind
friends said there were no black c
didn't argue. He didn't know of an
cowboys either. But he wished he c
cowboy sometimes.

Paul Stewart grew up. He became
He ran a shop in Denver, Colorado. H
liked hearing about cowboys. One day a
man came in. He was black. He had bee
cowboy. He talked of cattle drives he'd go
on.

Stewart listened to every word. He had m
one black cowboy. There must be more! He
decided to find out. He visited people's
homes. He talked to old people. He looked at
their pictures. He read their letters. Piece by
piece, Stewart began to put together a story. It
is the story of blacks in the American West.

Today Stewart runs the Black American
West Museum and Heritage Center in Denver.
About 3,000 people visit the museum each
year.

Stewart often speaks at schools about
blacks in the West. He tells of James
Beckwourth. The Crow Indians made
Beckwourth a chief. He talks of the Buffalo
Soldiers. They were a brave group of U.S.
cavalry.

He tells of Bill Pickett. Pickett was a
famous rodeo cowboy. He began the rodeo
event of throwing bulls. And he tells of Nat
Love. Love was a great shot. He won a
shooting contest in Deadwood, South Dakota.

107

...r that, they called him "Deadwood

...se, not all blacks in the West were
...Justina Ford was a doctor. She
... in Denver for 50 years.
...ll were good either. Some were
...s. Two black men rode with Jesse

...w you can read their stories. They are in
...Stewart's book, *Black Cowboys*. Stewart
...five more books planned. They will tell
...stories of other blacks in the West.

Questions

1. Fill in the blanks to tell the main idea about
   "Black Cowboys."

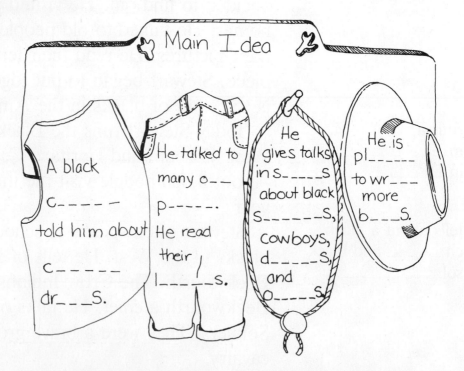

Main Idea

A black c _ _ _ _ _ told him about c _ _ _ _ _ dr_ _ _s.

He talked to many o_ _ p_ _ _ _ _. He read their l_ _ _ _s.

He gives talks in s_ _ _ _s about black s_ _ _ _ _ _s, cowboys, d_ _ _ _ _s, and o_ _ _ _s

He is pl_ _ _ _ _ to wr_ _ _ more b_ _ _s.

2. Which of the following is TRUE? Circle it.
   a. There were no black doctors in the West.
   b. In the West, black men were never outlaws.
   c. One black man became an Indian chief.

108

3. Why did people call Nat Love "Deadwood Dick"?

_____

_____

Think About It

Paul Stewart talked to people and looked at old pictures and letters to learn about life long ago. Think about one of your grandparents. Talk to your grandparent if you can. What was he or she doing at your age? How was his or her life different from your life now? Put your grandparent's name on the chart. Then fill in your ideas.

	My Life Now (Year: _____)	_____'s Life at My Age (Year: _____)
Family members		
Where home is		
Job or school		
Fun times		
Hopes and dreams		

Cultures: "Urban Legends, Part One"

Before You Read

Words to Know

Find these words in your word bank. Write their meanings here.

hitchhiking _____

_____

urban _____

_____

This story is about a hitchhiker. Have you ever

hitchhiked? _____

Would you ever pick up a hitchhiker? _____
Explain why you would or would not.

_____

_____

Now read Part One of "Urban Legends." Notice
that the story told in Part One is written the way a
person talks.

Urban Legends

Part One: The Vanishing Hitchhiker

People have always told legends. Legends are stories told out loud. Often the story is strange. But people believe it is true. "Robin Hood" is a very old legend.

People still tell stories today. Some of these stories are called "urban legends." *Urban* means "from the city." Urban legends are told mostly in cities and small towns.

An urban legend may be frightening. But it sounds like something that could happen to you. It often has a message or moral. It's always a good story.

Usually you're told, "This happened to a friend of a friend." But the same story shows up all over the country. *All* the stories can't be true!

Many of the best stories are about cars. Americans love cars. In a car, you can go far from home. You feel free. But there are dangers on the road. You may meet a stranger. Have you heard this story?

This happened to my friend's best friend and her father. They were driving home. It was in the country, on Highway 59. They saw a young girl by the road. She was hitchhiking. Well, they stopped to pick her up. She got in the back seat. She said she lived up the road. After that she didn't say a word. So they got to the house, and the father turned around. She was gone! The back seat was empty! The family went up to the door. They knocked. They told the people there what had happened. Well, the people said they had had a daughter. But she had disappeared years ago. She was last seen on that road. She had been hitchhiking. Today would have been her birthday.

Questions

1. What is one thing that is true about urban legends?
   a. They are told in a loud voice.
   b. They are always true.
   c. They are told in cities and towns.

2. This story is called "The Vanishing Hitchhiker." Think about what happens in the story. What do you think *vanishing* means?
   a. disappearing
   b. singing
   c. happy

3. Urban legends often have a *moral*. A moral tries to teach you about something. What could be a moral of this story?
   a. Don't hitchhike.
   b. Don't go out on your birthday.
   c. Don't drive in the country.

4. Who do you think the girl on the road was?

   _____

   _____

5. Do you think this story could be true? Explain.

Think About It

Do you know an urban legend? If you do, share the story with someone else.

Try to get some more urban legends from your friends. Decide if you think any of the stories are true.

Cultures: "Urban Legends, Part Two"

Before You Read

Look at the name of this story. What do you think the story will be about?

_____

_____

Now read to see what happens in Part Two of "Urban Legends." Notice that the story told in Part Two is written the way a person talks.

Urban Legends

Part Two: The Runaway Grandmother

What makes an urban legend? First, it is a good story. Second, it's told over and over. It tells about real places. Someone says, "This happened on the river." Or, "It was right by Rand Road." These names make it sound more real.

An urban legend never happened to the one telling it. That person heard it from another person. So you can never find out if it really happened.

People like to believe these stories. The stories show our hopes and fears. Often they are about death. They are also about modern life. They talk about cars, microwave ovens, and telephones.

One group of stories is about what happens when Grandma dies. The story is usually rather funny. But it shows how modern people feel about old age and death. Here's how one person told it.

There was this family. They were from Washington, I think. They drove to Mexico for vacation. There were the parents, two children, and Grandma. The grandmother rode in the back with the children. Well, they were having a good time. Then, one morning, the little girl cries out. "Daddy! Stop! I think Grandma is sick." They stop and look. The grandmother has died! Well, she was old. But still, it's a surprise. The children won't ride with Grandma. So they put her in a sleeping bag. They tie her on top of the car. And they drive to the next town. Then they look for a police station. They all go in to explain. And while they are in the station, some man steals their car. And Grandma.

Questions

1. What is one thing that is TRUE about urban legends?
   a. The person who is in the story is the one who tells what happened.
   b. The legends talk about places that are not real.
   c. The stories are about things that happen in modern life.

2. Why do they put Grandma on top of the car?

   _____

   _____

3. Why do they go to a police station?

   _____

   _____

4. What is one thing that the story tells you?
   a. how the man who stole the car felt
   b. where the family went on their trip
   c. where the family buried Grandma

 5. Do you think this story really happened? Explain why or why not.

Think About It

 You have read and talked about urban legends. Now, make up an urban legend of your own. Write down a few words about your story on the map. Then tell the story to someone else. Can you make that person think it is a true story?

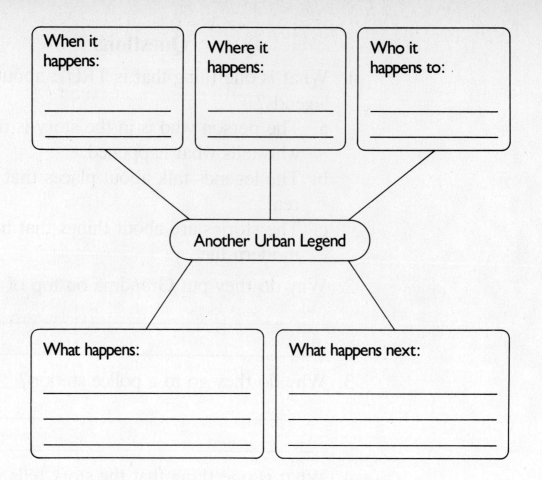

When it happens:	Where it happens:	Who it happens to:
_____	_____	_____
_____	_____	_____

Another Urban Legend

What happens:	What happens next:
_____	_____
_____	_____
_____	_____

Cultures: "Waiting for Rain"

Before You Read

A Word to Know

Find this word in your word bank. Write its meaning here.

accent   (AK sehnt) _____

_____

Read the first paragraph of the story. Picture what the day was like. How do *you* feel on days like that one?

_____

_____

As you read, see how the people in the story feel.

Waiting for Rain

It was a hot summer afternoon. All morning, it looked like rain. The sky got darker. The wind stopped. The smell of rain filled the air. You would think, "This is it. Now it will rain and cool off." But then, no rain. Just more heat.

I could not stand to be inside. It was even hotter there. So I took my baby and went out. We sat on the steps of our building, waiting for the rain.

We saw a lady come down the walk. She had a little dog. My baby was very happy to see the dog. She laughed and clapped her hands.

"Hello there," the lady said. She looked at the baby. "You are very pretty! What is your name?"

"Emily," I said, smiling.

"How old is she?" she asked.

"One year old, next month," I said.

"Oh, she is a big girl!" she said. I was very proud.

We talked awhile. Then the lady asked, "What are you? Did you grow up around here?"

"Yes," I said. "My folks live close by." But I knew that was not what the lady meant. Sometimes people hear an accent when I speak.

"What is your name?" she asked.

I told her my name. Paula Seibert. The last name sounds German. Then I added, "That is my husband's last name. I'm Mexican."

"Mexican?" the lady looked shocked. She was not so happy to be talking to me now. "But you don't look Mexican!"

"Sure I do," I said. "We come in all shades. There are plenty of people in Mexico who look like me."

I kept smiling at the lady. But I was very sad. I saw her turn to go. She pulled on the dog's leash.

Just then, it started to rain. Big, heavy drops. We both had an excuse to stop talking.

"Good-bye, Emily," she said as she walked away. She didn't turn around.

Emily and I went back upstairs. I carried her out on the porch. We watched the rain come. I rocked her for a long time out there.

Questions

1. Why was Paula sitting outside with her baby?
   a. They had no place to live.
   b. It was too hot inside.
   c. She wanted to meet people.

2. What did the lady mean when she said, "What are you?"
   a. What country do you come from?
   b. What do you do for a living?
   c. How are you?

3. How does the lady feel about Mexicans?

   _____

4. How can you tell the lady feels that way?

   _____

   _____

5. How do you think Paula felt at the end of the story?

   _____

   _____

Think About It

The weather changes in this story. People's feelings change too. On the chart, show how things change in "Waiting for Rain." Tell what things were like at the beginning of the story. Then tell what they were like at the end.

	What is the weather like?	How does Paula feel about the lady?	How does the lady feel about Paula?
at the beginning of the story			
at the end of the story			

Cultures: "Three Poems"

Before You Read

A Word to Know

Find this word in your word bank. Write its meaning here.

aches   (ayks) _____

_____

A Reading Tip   Look at the *ch* in *aches*. Does it make a soft *ch* sound, as in *child?* Or does it make a hard *k* sound? Try to say it both ways before you decide.

The next three poems are very short. Every word is important in a short poem. You may need to read the poem more than one time to understand it.

After you read these poems, read them again, out loud. Listen to the sounds of the words. Listen to the "beat" of each poem. See if the words rhyme or repeat.

As you read, picture what is happening in each poem.

Copyright © 1991 Scott, Foresman and Company.

Summer Grass by Carl Sandburg

Summer grass aches and whispers.

It wants something; it calls and sings; it pours
out wishes to the overhead stars.

The rain hears; the rain answers; the rain is slow
coming; the rain wets the face of the grass.

from Roofs and Stars by Cung Tram Tuong

Sad, I used to go up
on the fog-heavy roofs
roofs that stare in the evening
to write poems and reach for the stars.

Haiku by Onitsura

A cooling breeze—
and the whole sky is filled
with pine-tree voices.

Meet the Poets

Carl Sandburg was born in Illinois in 1878. When he
was 13, he left school to help his family. A few years
later, he went all around the country as a hobo. He
wrote many poems about life in America, from the
big cities to the quiet forests. He was known as "the
poet of the working people."

Copyright © 1991 Scott, Foresman and Company.

Cung Tram Tuong is a Vietnamese poet. Long ago, Vietnamese poets wrote in Chinese. Later, they used special signs to write poems in Vietnamese. Since the 1930s, Vietnamese poets have written in *chu nom*. *Chu nom* uses the letters from A to Z to write Vietnamese words.

Cung Tram Tuong wrote "Roofs and Stars" in *chu nom*. Another Vietnamese writer put the poem into English.

Onitsura lived in Japan from 1650 to 1738. He was one of the first people to write haiku poems.

Haiku poems are very short. They say something about a feeling or idea with just a few words. Onitsura's poems help the reader to see, hear, and feel the things he talks about.

Questions

1. What is the same about all three poems?
   a. They all rhyme.
   b. They are all by the same poet.
   c. They are all about the outdoors.

2. In "Summer Grass," what does the grass want?

_____

3. Imagine you are making a movie of "Summer Grass." What would you show?

4. In "Roofs and Stars," the poet talks about "fog-heavy roofs." How would you say this in your own words?

_____

_____

Copyright © 1991 Scott, Foresman and Company.

5. When does the poet go up on the roofs?
   a. when he is happy
   b. when he is unhappy
   c. when he gets up in the morning
6. In "Haiku," what is the poet talking about?
   a. the way the wind moves the tree branches
   b. the sound of a storm on a summer day
   c. people who are singing in the trees

Think About It

You have read many poems in this book. Look at them again. Which one do you like best?

_____

Tell what you like about it.

_____

_____

_____

Copyright © 1991 Scott, Foresman and Company.

Final Hints for Good Readers

In this book you have learned about different people, places, and ideas. You have also learned some different ways to become a better reader.

Here is a list of the keys to reading you have learned. Each time you read, remember these keys. They can help you!

Before You Read

- Look ahead at the reading. What is it about? Are there some facts you already know about it? Use those facts to better understand the reading.

- Think about *why* you are reading. Ask something you think the reading will answer.

As You Read

- Make guesses about what could happen next in the story.

- Try to picture how things look.

- Ask yourself about the reading. Do you understand what is happening?

- Don't read too slowly. Read in phrases.

After You Read

- Tell the main idea of the reading. Do you remember the most important details?

Copyright © 1991 Scott, Foresman and Company.

Looking Back

Word Bank

Look back at the word bank words on page 100. Do you still remember what they mean?

Choose five more words from Unit 4. Add the words and their meanings to your word bank.

Writing

Think of a culture you would like to know more about. If you could visit anywhere in the world, where would you go? Fill in your ideas on the map.

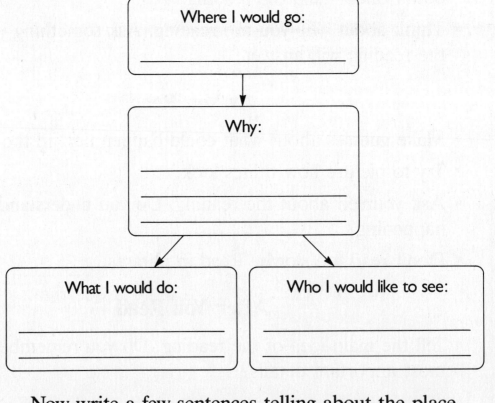

Now write a few sentences telling about the place you would like to visit. Use the ideas on the map.

_____

_____

Copyright © 1991 Scott, Foresman and Company.

End-of-Book Test:
"Wear a Helmet!"

Before You Read

Look at the name of this story. Can you guess what the story might be about? Write down your ideas.

_____

_____

Now read to see if you guessed right.

Copyright © 1991 Scott, Foresman and Company.

127

Wear a Helmet!

There is a strange man who hangs around by the library. His clothes are old and baggy. He limps. He has a wild look in his eyes.

I had seen this strange man often. He tries to stop people and talk to them. He tried to stop me a few times, but I got away. All I heard from him was, "I lost my wife. I lost my job. I have to tell you something . . . " I thought he was trying to pick me up. Or maybe he wanted money. Or maybe he was just crazy. I always got away from him real fast.

But one time I couldn't get away. I was waiting for a ride. The strange man saw me there. He came up to me. I pretended not to see him. But he still spoke to me.

"I lost my job. I lost my wife," he said.

"I'm so sorry," I said. I started to move away.

"You know why?" he asked. I didn't want to hear it. I stayed quiet. "I used to have a big job on Wall Street. I made a lot of money. I had a fine family. Then one day I was riding my bike. I didn't have a helmet on. A car hit me. I was in the hospital for a year. I lost my wife. I lost my job."

I had nothing to say. I was listening now. The man seemed so grateful to have somebody listen to him.

"So now I tell people to wear a helmet. If you ride a bike, just wear a helmet. If you don't, you might end up with a head like this."

He took off his old yellow cap. Through the scalp I saw a small plate shining.

"Oh, my God," I said. I felt so sorry.

But the man looked happy. He had made his point.

Copyright © 1991 Scott, Foresman and Company.

"So wear a helmet when you ride. Tell other people, too," he said. "God bless you."

He limped away. He wanted to tell more people. I saw him try a few, but no one stopped.

Questions

1. Why didn't the woman want to listen to the man?

   _____

   _____

   _____

2. Why did the man lose his job and his wife?
   a. He always tried to stop people and talk to them.
   b. His wife did not like his helmet.
   c. He was hit by a car.

3. Why does he want people to wear helmets?

   _____

   _____

4. What does the old man show the woman?
   a. pictures of his family
   b. his bike
   c. the plate in his head

5. At the end of the story, why was the old man happy?
   a. The woman had let him talk to her about wearing a helmet.
   b. He had a good job and a fine family.
   c. No one else wanted to talk to him.

6. How do you think the woman felt at the end of the story?

   _____

Copyright © 1991 Scott, Foresman and Company.

129

Just for Fun

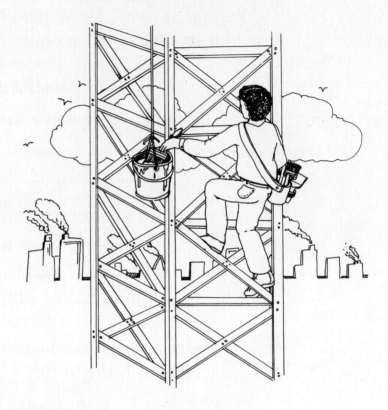

This story has no questions with it. It is for you to enjoy and think about. The story is longer than the other readings in this book. You are ready for a longer story because you have learned a lot about reading in this book.

Copyright © 1991 Scott, Foresman and Company.

Climbing High

I paint radio towers. Some people think it's easy. You just go up there and paint, they say. But they don't go up. I'm the one who climbs the tower. And I know it is not easy.

I learned to climb from the best. His name was Wayne. The day I met him, the lights had gone out. My father was away. My mother was afraid to touch anything.

I was no help. I could have fixed it. But I didn't want to. I was eighteen. I didn't want to do a thing. I had worked hard already. We had a hay farm. The hay was in.

So my mother called Wayne. We didn't know him. But they said he worked cheap. We didn't have much money.

He showed up an hour later. He didn't ring the bell. He just started unloading his truck. He was my father's age. He was not tall. But his back was strong. He whistled through his teeth. He worked quickly. "I'll be done in no time," he said.

"Give that man a hand," my mother said.

"I was going into town," I said. "I'll help him later."

"You help him now," she said.

I was going to talk back to her, but I didn't.

Wayne sized me up right away. "Just hand me my tools," he said.

I don't know what it was about Wayne. I was angry when we started. But after a while, I really liked being with him. He knew what he was doing. I wanted to show him that I knew too.

Copyright © 1991 Scott, Foresman and Company.

So I tried to do a good job. I gave him the right tools before he asked. "You're doing great, kid," he told me.

Wayne could see that I could have done the job. He could see that I needed a challenge. We got to talking.

"You got all your hay in?" Wayne asked me.

"Just yesterday," I said.

"Want to make some money? I need some help next Tuesday," he said.

"I guess so," I said. I wanted to make money. I just didn't want to work.

On Tuesday, Wayne came by for me. I thought we would go to a house. But we drove out into the woods. We went up a hill. At the top, there was an orange and white tower. Right away, I was worried.

"You don't have to go up," Wayne said.

"I'm not afraid," I lied.

Wayne knew that I was lying. But he didn't call me on it. Instead, he started to teach me. He showed me how to use the safety belt. He showed me all the tower tools. He showed me how to help him. In about three weeks, I was ready. Then Wayne taught me how to climb.

Being up there is like nothing else. It's so quiet. There is so much to see. And the work is like no other work I have done. You can't mess up, even once. You can't even drop a tool. You might kill someone.

But I loved it. I worked for Wayne for two years. He paid pretty good. He was always fair. I wanted to work for him forever. It was better than working the farm. I hated that. I let my brother do that now.

One day Wayne had bad news. He wasn't going to use me anymore. I was hurt. I didn't understand.

Copyright © 1991 Scott, Foresman and Company.

"You can't help me forever," he said. "You have to go off on your own. Start your own business."

"I don't know how to do that," I said.

"I'll help you," Wayne said. "I have more jobs than I can handle. I can give you some."

I had thought getting off the farm was a big deal. Now Wayne was pushing me farther. Could I really start a business?

"My legs are giving out," Wayne told me. "This is a young man's business."

I thought about it for weeks. Finally, I took him up on it.

I have been doing it for eight years now. There have been a few rough jobs. Like the time I climbed a tower near Dallas. I was higher than the tallest buildings. It took almost two hours just to get up there. I was nine hundred feet up. I worked for ten hours straight. I have never been so tired.

But I always go back up. It doesn't matter how bad the last job was. I'm just happy to be on my own, climbing high.

Copyright © 1991 Scott, Foresman and Company.

Answers

Copyright © 1991 Scott, Foresman and Company.

Unit 1 People

■ Somebody Gave Me a Chance page 7

1. Answers will vary. It's all right if your question was not answered. Asking any question helps you read the story better.

2. Thaison Nguyen lived in Vietnam during the war. He saw many American <u>airplanes</u>. He wanted to <u>fly</u> an airplane. After the war, Nguyen's family tried to <u>leave</u> Vietnam. They left on a boat. The American <u>navy</u> picked them up. The Nguyens came to America. Thaison went to school. He wanted to <u>join</u> the navy and learn to fly. It wasn't easy. But Nguyen is at the Naval Academy now. He says the United States is his <u>country</u>.

3. b. Nguyen was glad the navy had saved his family. Choice *a* is wrong because the story does not say he did not like the air force. Choice *c* is wrong because the navy did not ask

him to join. He had to work hard to get in the navy.

4. Answers will vary. The story says the senators were moved by what Nguyen said.

5. Answers will vary. Since the United States has helped his family, Nguyen probably likes this country very much.

■ Starting Over—at 95 page 13

1. Almost everyone in Omaha knows Rose Blumkin. They <u>call</u> her "Mrs. B." For many years, she and her husband sold <u>furniture</u>. Even after their store was sold, the family still <u>worked</u> there. Then the family had a <u>fight</u>. Mrs. B left. But she was <u>unhappy</u>. She decided to do something about it. At 95, Mrs. B <u>opened</u> her own store.

2. Answers will vary. She may have felt sad and angry.

3. Answers will vary.

4. Answers will vary. It makes sense to say she is hardworking and brave.

135

■ We Real Cool   page 17

1. The word "we" is used over and over.

2. c. At the beginning of the poem it says, "The Pool Players."

3. Answers will vary. "We are great" is another way to say it.

4. a. no. The poem says, "We left school." **b.** yes. The poem says, "We lurk late." **c.** yes. The poem says, "We sing sin."

5. pool, June, soon

6. Answers will vary. Some words are *spoon, moon,* and *tune.*

■ Lester Rasmussen: Jane's Blue Jeans   page 20

1. a. Lester says Jane's blue jeans are "the saddest blue" he's seen all day. Choice *b* is wrong because Lester never sees Jane in the poem. Choice *c* is wrong because it's the blue jeans that make Lester sad more than the rain.

2. The poem says they are torn, faded, and in the shape of Jane.

3. c. The poem says that Jane is now "in another pair of blue jeans." Choice *a* is wrong because the poem does not say Jane has died. Choice *b* is wrong because the poem does not tell if she loves Lester or not.

4. Answers will vary. Jane's blue jeans probably make Lester sad because he would like to see Jane, not just her blue jeans.

■ Larry Graham: Empty Beer Can Estelle Etherege: Fifty   page 23

1. a. He says "you don't love me anymore," so he is probably talking to his girlfriend.

2. Answers will vary. His sister and his boss would probably not write to him and say they don't love him anymore.

3. b. The poem says she threw a beer can out the window of his pickup. Choices *a* and *c* are wrong because they happened later.

4. Answers will vary. She threw both of them away.

5. c. We know it is Estelle's birthday because she says, "Today, I am fifty years old."

6. It is falling apart. The porch sags, a window is broken, and the paint is peeling.

7. c. The numbers begin with 51, not 1, so we can tell she is counting the years she has left.

8. Answers will vary. She does not seem happy about her birthday. She

Copyright © 1991 Scott, Foresman and Company.

136

talks about her house being in sad shape, but she might be talking about herself too.

■ Out on a Limb   page 27

1. b. The speaker says she went out on a limb for a person she didn't even know. Then she tells about Betty. Choice *a* is wrong because the story does not say she tried to do the hardest job. Choice *c* is wrong because the story does not say she went back to school.

2. Betty was not smart. People thought she was strange. But she was a good worker.

3. They thought she was strange.

4. c. The story says the boss saw that other people stayed away from Betty. They made fun of her. Then he decided to fire her.

5. He fired her for trying to help Betty.

■ José Venzor   page 30

1. Answers will vary. It's all right if your question was not answered. Asking any question will help you read the story better.

2. a. Because he went to church, he learned to love <u>pictures</u>. **b.** Because he wanted a job, he moved to <u>Wisconsin</u>. **c.** Because he went into the army, he learned to <u>cook</u>. **d.** Because he opened a pizzeria, he made lots of <u>money</u>. **e.** Because he loves art, he opened an <u>art gallery</u>.

3. a. yes; **b.** yes; **c.** no. The story says he learned to cook in the army, not in the homes.

4. Answers will vary.

■ People Learning to Read   page 34

1. Answers will vary.

2. c. The story says Mr. Guice wanted to have his own shop. Choice *a* is wrong because Mr. Guice already knew how to fix cars. Choice *b* is wrong because the story says Mr. Guice went back to school for three years to learn to read.

3. a. The story talks about the extra things adults must deal with, like jobs and children. Choice *b* is wrong because nothing is said about children having more problems in school. Choice *c* is also wrong because it does not tell why learning to read is *different* for adults and children.

4. Answers will vary. Possible reasons: People may have had a bad time at school as children. They may have had problems seeing letters.

5. Answers will vary. Since O. D. Guice got his own shop, learning to read probably helped him.

Copyright © 1991 Scott, Foresman and Company.

137

Unit 2   Coping

■ Learning New Words
page 38

1. b. If Malcolm was sick, his parents were probably <u>worried</u> about his health. They would not be bored or happy.

2. c. If no one sees you behind the chair, you must have bent over or stooped low. Choice *a* is wrong because to bite *something* would not make sense here. Choice *b* is wrong because if you jumped over something, people would see you.

3. a. If babies are interested in everything, it makes sense to say they want to know things. It does not make sense to say they get angry quickly or have problems, so *b* and *c* are wrong.

4. b. When Jeff puts the names of new patients into a computer, he is putting facts into a computer. The sentences do not say he takes care of patients, so *a* is wrong. They do not say he sells computers, so *c* is wrong.

5. a. It makes sense to say, "When my daughter does something bad, I *punish* her by making her stay in her room."

6. a. If Nathan is watching his boss and learning from him, it makes sense to say he is trying to be like him.

7. b. If Ricky's clothes are too tight, he must be *heavier* than before. Being *fast* would not make Ricky's clothes tighter, so *a* is wrong. If he were *taller,* his clothes would be too short, not too tight, so *c* is wrong.

■ José Cruz   page 42

1. c. In the poem, he talks about putting the bar over his head. He says, "Put on more weights." He is talking about how much weight he wants to lift.

2. b. The poem says that when he feels the weight of the world, he goes to the gym and thinks about nothing. It makes sense to say he feels the weight of his problems and goes to the gym to forget them.

3. He goes to the gym to feel good about himself. He can forget about school, his life, and his future for a while.

4. He thinks about nothing.

138

Copyright © 1991 Scott, Foresman and Company.

■ Five Ways to Stay Healthy page 48

1. You should exercise two or three times a week.

2. Cake, candy, and other sweets are not good for you. They make you gain weight.

3. Yes. The chart says a man who is 5'6" tall should weigh between 133 and 163 pounds. If he weighs 166 pounds, he is too heavy.

4. The chart shows that **c** is correct.

■ When Someone Is Choking page 51

1. You can help someone who is choking. First, stand <u>behind</u> the person. Give four hard blows on the person's <u>back</u>. If that does not work, make a <u>fist</u> with one hand. Put your fist above the other person's <u>waist</u>. Cover your fist with your other <u>hand</u>. Then <u>pull</u> up and in with your fist. Do this four <u>times</u>. If the person is still choking, repeat the <u>blows</u> on the back.

2. c. If the person turns blue, it means he or she can't take a breath.

3. Answers will vary.

■ Can Your Child Kick Drugs? page 55

1. Answers will vary. Three things that can happen are: 1) the child will want drugs all the time; 2) the child will breathe quickly; 3) the child will have hot flashes and chills.

2. a. The reading says that when children have problems kicking drugs, they need outside help. It can be too much for you to handle alone.

3. Answers will vary. You can talk to your child. You can try to keep your child away from friends who take drugs. You can show the child your love.

4. You can call a hot line, look in the telephone book, or call a hospital.

■ Woman Work page 58

1. Answers will vary. Some of the other words that rhyme are *mop* and *shop, fry* and *dry, sick* and *pick.*

2. Answers will vary. Three of the things she has to do are mend clothes, mop the floor, and feed company.

3. b. She says, "Storm, blow me from here . . . . 'Til I can rest again."

4. Answers will vary.

■ Some Tips for Parents page 61

1. Answers will vary. It's all right if your question was not answered. Asking any question will help you read the story better.

2. If you don't listen, your child may stop wanting to learn about things.

Copyright © 1991 Scott, Foresman and Company.

3. All children are different. Your children should feel they are special.

4. c. The reading says it is *not* good to keep your child too busy. It says children need time to dream.

5. Answers will vary.

■ Do Your Homework!   page 66

1. c. Anita was worried about buying clothes and taking care of her daughter. She did want to work, so *a* is wrong. She was ready to be a data entry clerk, so *b* is also wrong.

2. The bank gave Anita a computer and telephone line so she could work at home.

3. a. 3; **b.** 2; **c.** 4; **d.** 1.

4. She can be with her daughter. Also, she doesn't have to buy new clothes.

Unit 3   Messages

■ Justin Faust   page 73

1. his parents' divorce

2. Answers will vary. Possible answer: The nights and the weekends are hard to get through.

3. c. The poem does *not* say Justin's father is happier, so *b* is wrong. It does say that Justin's mother cries at night, but not his father, so *a* is wrong. It says Justin talks to his father on the telephone, so *c* is correct.

4. He wishes his parents would speak to each other.

■ Navajo Code-Talkers   page 79

1. Answers will vary.

2. so the enemy could not understand them

3. a. The Navajo speak Athapaskan.

4. b. The reading says the code-talkers spoke another code in Athapaskan. Choice *a* is wrong because the Japanese did break all the other codes except Athapaskan. These codes would also be top secret. Choice *c* is wrong because the Japanese did break the other radio codes.

5. c. No one could talk about the Navajo code-talkers until 1968.

6. He was sorry people had insulted the Navajo during the war. He was sorry no one knew how brave they had been.

■ Dear Abby   page 83

1. b. She does not ask for money, so *a* is wrong. She tells people how hard her life is, so *c* is wrong.

2. b. She goes to school during the day, so *a* is wrong. She doesn't have time to go out with friends, so *c* is wrong.

Copyright © 1991 Scott, Foresman and Company.

3. Six hours. She goes to bed at 11 p.m. and gets up at 5 a.m.

4. Answers will vary. Some things she would need are diapers, formula, baby food, baby clothes, medicine, her schoolbooks, her clothes, and money for gas or for the bus.

5. Answers will vary.

■ The Dog's Tale   page 87

1. a beer

2. They sound like a dog barking.

3. b. The first words the dog says all sound like barking.

4. Babe Ruth. Babe Ruth was a great baseball player who played for the New York Yankees.

5. a. The dog gives the bartender the name of another great baseball player.

■ Primer Lesson Deceased page 90

1. a. The poem teaches something people should learn as early as possible.

2. b. The poem says it is not easy to call proud words back. It does not say you get what you want, so *a* is wrong. It does not say people like you more, so *c* is wrong.

3. Answers will vary.

4. a letter

5. c. The name of the poem is a clue to the answer.

6. because the person is dead

7. Answers will vary. The person probably feels sad and empty.

■ Bad Fight, Good Fight page 94

1. b. Rita wants to go out and have fun after work.

2. a. Dan is tired from working hard all day.

3. a. Dan goes out and Rita stays home and cries, so *b* and *c* are wrong.

4. They both feel bad.

5. Answers will vary. One thing they could do is tell how they feel about things.

6. Answers will vary. Fighting can help people learn more about each other's feelings.

Unit 4   Cultures

■ Word Bank Puzzle   page 100

Down

1. cattle drives
2. outlaws
3. hitchhiking
4. urban

Across

5. accent
6. aches
7. rodeo

Copyright © 1991 Scott, Foresman and Company.

■ High on Lowriding   page 103

1. **a.** yes; **b.** yes; **c.** no. The story says that lowriders are cars, so *a* is right. It says the people who make them are called lowriders, too, so *b* is right. Choice *c* is wrong because bicycles are not called lowriders.

2. **b.** The story tells a lot about how fancy the cars are, so *b* is the best answer. It does not talk about how dangerous they are, so *a* is wrong. It does not say they are cheap, so *c* is wrong.

3. Answers will vary. They are probably called "lowriders" because they ride so low on the ground.

4. Answers will vary.

■ Black Cowboys   page 108

1. **Main Idea:** Paul <u>Stewart</u> <u>learned</u> a lot about blacks in the <u>West</u>. Now he <u>tells</u> their <u>story</u> to other <u>people</u>. **Details:** A black <u>cowboy</u> told him about <u>cattle drives</u>. He talked to many <u>old people</u>. He read their <u>letters</u>. He gives talks in <u>schools</u> about black <u>soldiers</u>, cowboys, <u>doctors</u>, and <u>outlaws</u>. He is <u>planning</u> to <u>write</u> more <u>books</u>.

2. **c.** The Crow Indians made James Beckwourth a chief. Choice *a* is wrong because the reading says Justina Ford was a doctor. Choice *b* is wrong because the reading says two

black men were outlaws with Jesse James.

3. because he won a shooting contest in Deadwood, South Dakota

■ Urban Legends,
   Part One
   page 112

1. **c.** The reading says that urban legends are told mostly in cities and small towns.

2. **a.** The hitchhiker *disappears* while she is riding with the family.

3. **a.** The parents lost their daughter after she hitchhiked. The story warns people that it can be dangerous to hitchhike.

4. Answers will vary. She was probably the ghost of the daughter who disappeared while hitchhiking.

5. Answers will vary.

■ Urban Legends,
   Part Two
   page 115

1. **c.** Choice *a* is wrong because the reading says a legend is never told by the person the things happened to. Choice *b* is wrong because it says urban legends talk about real places.

2. because the children don't want to ride next to her body

3. to tell the police that Grandma has died

142

Copyright © 1991 Scott, Foresman and Company.

4. b. The story does not tell us how the man felt when he found Grandma on top of the car. It does say the family went to Mexico, so *b* is correct. The family did not bury Grandma, so *c* is wrong.

5. Answers will vary.

■ Waiting for Rain page 119

1. b. She said it was so hot inside she went outside with her baby.

2. a. The lady heard her accent. She wanted to know what country she was from.

3. She does not like Mexicans.

4. She doesn't look happy when she finds out Paula is Mexican. She walks away.

5. Answers will vary. She probably felt sad.

■ Three Poems page 123

1. c. The poems do not rhyme, so *a* is wrong. They are by three different poets, so *b* is wrong.

2. the rain

3. Answers will vary.

4. Answers will vary. Possible answer: roofs covered with fog.

5. b. The poet says he would go up on the roofs when he was sad.

6. a. The pine-tree voices are the sound of the wind in the pine trees.

■ End-of-Book Test: Wear a Helmet! page 129

1. She thought he was trying to pick her up. He looked strange. She thought he wanted money or was crazy.

2. c. He lost his job and his wife after a year in the hospital.

3. so they don't end up like him

4. c. He takes off his cap and shows her the plate in his head.

5. a. Choice *b* is wrong because he does not have a good job or a family. Choice *c* is wrong because he would not be happy that others would not talk to him.

6. Answers will vary. She probably felt sorry for him and glad that she had listened.

Copyright © 1991 Scott, Foresman and Company.

To the Teacher

The *Foundations* Series

The *Foundations for Adult Reading* series was designed to do just what the name states: lay a sound basis for reading comprehension in adult new readers. It can be used on its own, as the core text in a reading program that takes a whole-language approach. It can also be used as part of a beginning reading program that includes decoding instruction. The books assume students have an understanding of sound-symbol relationships, some decoding ability, and a basic sight-word reading vocabulary. This section provides information and suggests activities for teachers working one-on-one with students as well as in a group situation.

High-Interest Readings on Adult Topics

The focus of the *Foundations* series is on building comprehension by reading high-interest stories and using effective reading strategies. Each book is organized around four themes: People, Coping, Messages, and Cultures.

Unit 1, "People," depicts the life experiences of real and fictional people. The variety of people represented reflects the multiethnic, multiracial nature of our society. Many of the people described are working to make their lives better.

Unit 2, "Coping," provides insights into how people cope with the variety of problems in contemporary life, from health to raising children to finding a job.

The readings in Unit 3, "Messages," have to do with communication. Some readings, such as "Justin Faust," are about how communication can break down in a family. Others, like "Dear Abby," are about people who have a message to share with the rest of us. A few readings, such as "The Dog's Tale," are just for fun.

The last unit, "Cultures," offers fictional and real-life stories that express the richness of the world's many cultures. Some readings, such as the three poems, are taken from the art of traditional cultures. Other readings—especially the urban legends and the article on "lowriding"—deal with popular culture. Your students may have some fun with these stories!

Copyright © 1991 Scott, Foresman and Company.

Readability

Some people feel readability formulas are helpful in assessing materials; others do not. The Spache readability formula was one of many factors used to assess the lessons and reading passages in the *Foundations* books. Using the Spache formula, the approximate grade-equivalent reading level for *Foundations for Adult Reading 1* is mid first grade. The approximate grade-equivalent reading level for *Foundations for Adult Reading 2* is early second grade.

Readability formulas can be useful tools for comparing reading material, as long as they are understood to be only rough guidelines. Assigning a grade level to reading material for adults can be misleading, because adults are not at the same developmental level and do not have the same oral vocabulary as children. Whether a particular reading will be understood depends to a large degree on the background knowledge the reader brings to the text. Grade levels, therefore, are a factor in evaluating the readability of a book, but certainly not the only factor.

Readability was also improved in the *Foundations* books by keeping lessons brief, breaking up text with illustrations, and designing the books with beginning adult readers in mind. The clarity of the writing style and the appeal of the subject matter also help determine the difficulty or ease with which a reader handles written material. The *Foundations* books offer a wide variety of subjects and themes. You may want to give students choices by letting them decide which reading passages or units to read.

Foundations and the *Adult Reading Comprehension* Series

Once students have completed the two *Foundations* books, you have the option of continuing their reading development with Scott, Foresman's *Adult Reading Comprehension* series. The themes in *Foundations*—People, Coping, Messages, and Cultures—are carried forward in *Adult Reading Comprehension,* as are the focus on building reading comprehension and the development of critical thinking.

Teaching Reading Strategies with *Foundations*

Reading comprehension is a holistic process, not merely a composite of isolated skills. Comprehension improves as students develop strategies for approaching unfamiliar text. As these strategies become automatic, students become successful readers—regardless of whether they are reading

Copyright © 1991 Scott, Foresman and Company.

146

on a second-grade level or a college level. A student who is a successful reader can read a story at his or her appropriate grade level, get meaning from it, respond to it, and add that meaning to a general framework of knowledge.

Foundations 1 encourages students to become "active readers"—readers who actively construct meaning from the text and respond to it in some way. The book teaches seven strategies and follows them up throughout the book.

The strategies taught in *Foundations 1* are described below, along with a listing of the pages on which they appear. Suggestions for teaching these strategies follow the descriptions.

Setting Your Own Purpose

(pp. 4, 28, 59)

A good reader is able to articulate reasons for reading. Usually a reader's purpose is to find out something. Sometimes it is simply to enjoy a good story. Having a purpose for reading helps motivate the reader because it gives each reader a personal commitment to comprehending the selection. It also helps focus the reader's attention.

The strategy lesson "Thinking About *Why* You Read" on page 4 asks students to reflect on the many reasons they may have for reading. Students preview an article on a Vietnamese refugee and are guided through the thinking process that leads to setting a purpose for reading the article. The "Before You Read" section of some other selections follows up on this strategy by asking students what they want to learn from a selection.

Picturing What You Read

(pp. 18, 19–21, 22, 117, 121)

Much has been written about the benefits of visualization techniques in areas ranging from finance to sports. For the beginning adult reader, creating a vivid picture while reading is a way to make text more meaningful and enjoyable. Readers are also more likely to notice their comprehension errors if those errors interfere with or contradict an image they have mentally constructed.

In the strategy lesson "Picturing What You Read" on page 18, students are encouraged to form a picture in their minds by noticing details about what is seen in several poems. Sidenotes in the accompanying poems ask students to describe to themselves what is happening in each scene.

Copyright © 1991 Scott, Foresman and Company.

Using What You Know

(pp. 25, 32, 44, 53, 92, 106, 110, 117)

The beginning adult reader is far more likely to experience success with readings on familiar topics. By "using what they know," adult students can tap into the wealth of their personal experience.

However, some students are unable to make the connection between their personal knowledge and their reading. They may read a baseball story without ever applying what they already know about baseball to the story.

The strategy lesson "Using What You Know" on page 44 helps adult readers develop this ability by making the connection between prior knowledge and comprehension. Before reading a selection about staying healthy, students add what they already know about staying healthy to a word map. This strategy is followed up with mapping and listing activities in the "Before You Read" section of other selections as well.

Making Predictions Before You Read

(pp. 4, 41, 49, 50, 59, 72, 77, 81, 101, 113, 127)

Making predictions allows a reader to become actively engaged with the text. When readers begin to think about what an article could be about, or what event could take place next in a story, they have a stronger purpose for reading and, thus, greater motivation to comprehend.

Emphasize to students that their predictions will not always be correct. Perhaps not enough information was given in the beginning for a good prediction. Or perhaps an author has deliberately misled the reader to create suspense. Remind students that the purpose of making predictions is to learn to look for clues about the topic of a reading and to think about the reading as it is being read.

The strategy lesson "Thinking Ahead" on page 49 encourages students to make "good guesses" about the topic of a story or article. The "Before You Read" section for some selections also asks students to make predictions about the reading.

Reading in Phrases

(pp. 62–64)

One obstacle for many beginning readers is their tendency to deal with only one word at a time, progressing so slowly that by the time they finish, they lose the overall sense of a passage. Learning to read in phrases is a very useful strategy for these students.

In the strategy lesson "Reading in Phrases" on pages 62–63, students are asked to observe the way spoken language naturally breaks into phrases. Next, they put lines after phrases in sentences from an upcoming story. In the selection that follows, students practice breaking up the

Copyright © 1991 Scott, Foresman and Company.

text into meaningful phrases. Tell your students that there is no one "right" way to divide sentences into phrases. The important thing is to learn to read in meaningful groups of words.

Asking Yourself Questions

(pp. 4, 28, 59, 75–76, 77)

Asking questions is another way readers become actively involved with a text. Readers who formulate questions before, during, and after reading are more likely to comprehend and recall the details of the reading. This may include questions about what is happening in a story or article, why it happens, how it is related to what the reader already knows, and what it means personally to the reader.

The strategy lesson "Asking Yourself Questions" on pages 75–76 highlights the importance of asking questions about a reading. In the selection that follows, students are asked to formulate a question before reading the story and to report on the answer afterwards. Other selections also ask students to write down questions before reading.

Finding the Main Idea

(pp. 104–105, 106–108)

Approaching main idea as a strategy rather than as an isolated skill encourages greater independence in beginning adult readers. With a strategies approach, readers are taught that identifying the main idea of a reading is a tool for understanding and remembering what is read.

This strategy is a crucial one for beginning adult readers, who may not be able to distinguish between relevant and irrelevant information. To reinforce the concept that recognizing the main idea is a tool, rather than an end in itself, use "real" text instead of isolated paragraphs. For example, students could bring in news articles for discussions on how finding the main idea can help them better understand the articles.

The strategy lesson "Finding the Main Idea" on pages 104–105 provides a visual explanation of the relationship between the main idea and supporting details. In the story that follows, students are asked to identify the main idea of each paragraph and of the entire selection.

Teaching Reading Strategies

As you guide students through *Foundations 1,* the following techniques will help you teach these strategies:

1. *Direct instruction.* The first time a strategy appears in *Foundations 1,* explain *what* it is, *how* it is helpful, and *when* it should be applied. Relate each strategy to examples from "real world" reading material—

Copyright © 1991 Scott, Foresman and Company.

newspapers, magazines, job application forms, etc. When students read these materials, remind them of strategies that may help their comprehension.

2. *Teacher modeling.* As you move through the book, you can review strategies by *modeling* them for students.

Modeling is a four-step process. In the first step, you name the strategy and relate its usefulness to a concrete experience in the students' lives. In the second step, you define the strategy and model it by "thinking out loud" for the students. In step three, you assist students as they practice applying the strategy to another example. In step four, students practice the strategy independently.

Here is an example of a teacher modeling the "Asking Yourself Questions" strategy (pp. 75–76) after reading "Dear Abby" on pages 81–82.

Step 1 Suppose you saw a newspaper article with this headline: "Woman Gives Birth on Subway Train." If you decided to read the article, you would probably have some questions. Can you think of some questions you'd ask yourself? First, you'd probably want to know why the woman was on a subway train and not at the hospital! Then you might ask, "Did the other passengers help her? Is she all right? Is the baby all right?" You would read the article to find the answers.

Step 2 When you ask yourself questions about what you read, you understand and remember it better. I'll show you what I mean. Let's imagine I haven't read the "Dear Abby" letter. What questions could I ask about the letter before I read it? Let's see. The title says, "Dear Abby, I'm a 16-Year-Old Single Mom." I wonder why she's writing to Abby. Does she have a problem she wants Abby to solve? That can be one of my questions. As I read this letter, I'm going to look for the answer.

After I read the letter, I know the answer to my question. She's writing to Abby to tell others what it's like being a teenaged mother.

Step 3 Now, can you think of another question I could ask about this story as I read it? (Possible answer: Who takes care of her son while she's at school?)

Step 4 OK, now it's your turn. Look at "The Dog's Tale" on pages 86–87. Look at the title. What are some questions you can ask yourself about the reading? (Possible question: Is the dog telling the story?) When you finish, check to see if your questions are answered.

As students learn the different strategies, encourage them to make decisions about which strategies to use. Emphasize that expert readers are flexible in deciding which strategies will be most helpful in a given situation. You can also extend their understanding by modeling strategies with materials students bring in to read.

Copyright © 1991 Scott, Foresman and Company.

Using *Foundations 1* in Your Classroom

Foundations 1 was developed to involve your students in the whole of language—in reading, speaking, listening, and writing. You can use the book to have your students read and think about interesting topics, talk about the ideas they've read about, and write about those ideas.

Reading

The "Before You Read" sections guide students through prereading strategies. Stress the importance of these prereading strategies. You can use the analogy of swimming: A swimmer wouldn't just dive into a pool headfirst without first checking the depth of the water. In the same way, a good reader doesn't just "dive" into reading material without first "testing the water" by looking at the titles and pictures, determining the topic, thinking of what he or she already knows about the topic, and so on.

Use the prereading strategies discussed in each "Before You Read" section as a starting point; expand on these strategies whenever possible. Ask students what they know about the topic beforehand, and try to relate the topic to students' interests.

Some readings or parts of readings may be too difficult for certain students. Pay attention to how students react to these readings in particular: "José Venzor," "Can Your Child Kick Drugs?," and "Urban Legends." These readings contain special vocabulary that may make them more difficult to read. Students may also experience difficulty reading about topics they have little knowledge of. In such cases, you can read to the students while they follow along.

Guided reading is another method you can use with certain selections. Have students read a section or even just a paragraph at a time. Then ask specific questions about what they have read. Ask whether they have any questions. Also ask students to predict what will happen next. Discuss previous predictions and whether they were correct. Then have students read the next section or paragraph. Continue this way through the entire selection.

Guided reading is also a good way to address the communicative nature of punctuation. Stress to students that the author of the selection is using punctuation marks to tell them when to pause (comma) or stop (period) and when to "hear" a question being asked (question mark) or a statement being said strongly (exclamation point). Marks of punctua-

151

Copyright © 1991 Scott, Foresman and Company.

tion can even help students hear someone's exact words (quotation marks).

Avoid having students read aloud in front of others, unless they volunteer to do so. Adult readers are often extremely sensitive about their reading ability. It's best to limit such oral reading to private diagnostic sessions with yourself.

Some readings include simple charts. Help your students interpret these charts. Show them how the chart is organized and how to read a chart to gain information.

Writing

Writing abilities may be quite limited in students at this level. Some may not be able to do the writing activities suggested in the book. You are in the best position to decide on an individual basis whether to assign such activities and to whom.

If a student cannot respond in writing, you can have the student dictate his or her answers for you to write down. Then the student can read the answers back. This sort of language experience activity would be especially useful with the critical thinking questions under "Think About It."

When students do write their answers, try to emphasize the ideas they have communicated and not mechanics such as spelling or capitalization. Beginning writers are often reluctant writers because they fear making mistakes in grammar or spelling; you can help students overcome their hesitation by postponing instruction in the mechanics of English until they feel more at ease when they write.

Working in pairs is one way to overcome uneasiness about writing and help foster a cooperative learning atmosphere. Having students work in pairs to write their answers may remove the tension over making a mistake and create friendly, helpful peer relationships. However, be sensitive to individual personalities when trying this technique. Some adults prefer to work alone and may be uncomfortable writing in pairs.

Speaking and Listening

Questions in the book marked with the symbol of a speaking person are meant to be answered orally. These questions are best answered verbally either because the answer is too involved for students to write out or because there is more than one right answer (or no "right" answer).

When students are verbally answering involved questions, write their answers on the board or an overhead transparency. Note words students use in their speaking vocabularies that they do not have in their reading

Copyright © 1991 Scott, Foresman and Company.

vocabularies. You may want students to add these words to their word banks.

When students are answering questions with no clearcut answers, you can use the questions as discussion topics. If you are working with a group of students, group discussions can make the readings come alive. Using small-group or class discussion in this way increases students' interest and adds variety to classroom routine.

Make sure students understand the question. Set a time limit for discussion. If you are dividing the class into small groups, a group size between three and six students is good. Assign or have each group select a spokesperson to share the group's ideas with the class.

Not all students are able to keep up with a group discussion. Some adults do not comprehend oral information that comes flooding in quickly from several sources. They may also become lost or confused when several people talk at once or in quick succession. You can help such students by joining their group and keeping an ongoing list of the main points of the discussion on a chalkboard or flip chart.

Building Vocabulary

Foundations 1 stresses vocabulary development through use of context clues while reading and through building a word bank. Try to give sufficient time to "Making a Word Bank" in Unit 1 and the first lesson of each unit after that ("Learning New Words," "Using Clues to Read New Words," and "Word Bank Puzzle"). Each should take a whole lesson in itself to help ensure that students develop this difficult but valuable reading strategy.

The "Words to Know" section before each selection and the word banks students create with these words help increase their sight vocabulary. You can work with these tools.

Develop a speaking and reading familiarity with the words in "Words to Know" in these ways.

▪ Say the words so that students know how to pronounce them.

▪ Ask students if they can use the words in sentences, and write their responses on the board or an overhead transparency.

▪ The definition given for each word in "Words to Know" is the meaning it has in the story that follows. Talk with students about other meanings a word might have.

Encourage students to add words they read and hear to their word banks, in addition to the words in "Words to Know." You can use students' word banks as a resource for vocabulary activities such as these:

Copyright © 1991 Scott, Foresman and Company.

153

- Write meanings for the words on cards and have students match the words with their definitions.

- Create cloze exercises by writing a sentence for each word with a blank where the word belongs, and have students pick the card with the word that fits in the blank.

- Have students work in pairs and use their word banks as flash cards.

- Ask students to sort their words into different categories. For example, have them classify the words according to their initial letters, and teach the sounds of initial consonants. Next, have students sort the cards into spelling patterns (such as words with *ea* or words with long vowel sounds and final silent *e*'s), and teach these sound patterns. Then have students sort the words according to their referents (such as "things" and "people").

Testing Comprehension

The questions after each reading selection will help you measure students' comprehension—both literal and inferential—of the material they have just read. As noted before, you can have students write their answers or dictate the answers to you. You can also help students compose their answers or model answers for them. Some multiple-choice questions have been included because they are often easier for writing-reluctant students to answer. Questions to be answered orally can be handled individually, in small groups, or as a class.

Some questions—those requiring inference or application—depend on the ability to "read between the lines" or use one's background knowledge. Help students understand that the answer isn't always "right there" on the page; they must sometimes think about what they've read, put different parts of the material together to draw a conclusion, or use what they already know to answer a question. There are several methods for teaching strategies for answering questions—analyzing the relationship between question and answer and figuring out how to locate the answer. The QAR approach is one such method.

With QAR (Question Answer Relationships) you help students analyze whether the answer to a question is "in the book" or "in my head." If it is "in the book," students must find it "right there" (in one sentence on the page) or "put it together" (take different text parts to find it). If the answer is "in my head," students must determine whether the needed information is between the "author and me" (take information the author gives you and infer from it) or whether it can be found "on my own" (take information from your experience and knowledge and apply it). If you are interested in learning more about the QAR

Copyright © 1991 Scott, Foresman and Company.

approach, see Taffy Raphael's article listed in the bibliography at the end of this section. You can use the reading selections and questions to develop in your students such question-answering strategies as these and thereby further students' reading comprehension.

Whole-Language Activities with the *Foundations* Books

The *Foundations* books are excellent resources for use in whole-language teaching. The following activities may be used with the books to infuse whole-language learning into your tutorial or classroom instruction.

Fostering Interaction

To break the ice so that the talk and ideas flow during instruction, you may want to try the following activities.

▪ **The Warm-Up** Before reading a selection, read and talk about short, digestible bits of print that are related to it. For example, a notice about cholesterol screening could be a warm-up for "Five Ways to Stay Healthy" on pages 46–47. Even the nutrition information on a food package would do. Read the print. Talk about it. Break the ice and encourage your students to start thinking about what they will read.

Jokes, cartoons, sayings, newspaper clippings, short poems, photos, commercials, or "tidbits" from the book may be used as warm-ups. You can read these to your students or take turns reading with them—whatever is most comfortable and natural.

▪ **Old Favorites** Just because you read something once doesn't mean you have to be done with it. Occasionally have your students select favorite stories, poems, or portions of articles to reread. You can use this as an opportunity to discuss the selection in greater detail, pointing out certain features of language. For example, if your students choose to reread their favorite poems from *Foundations 1,* discuss the words that helped them create mental pictures. Explore synonyms and antonyms for these high-image words. Add some to the word bank.

Or if your students choose to reread a selection about a successful person, ask them to describe the qualities and character traits that may have contributed to the person's success. Have them relate the list to themselves or people they know. You can also use these new ideas to expand the word maps that were developed in earlier lessons.

Copyright © 1991 Scott, Foresman and Company.

155

Facilitating Involvement

You can show your adult learners what successful readers do while reading by involving them in these strategies.

▪ **Reciprocal Questioning** When you use this strategy, you and your students take turns asking each other questions about the first few paragraphs of a selection. Begin by explaining that everyone will read the first paragraph of a selection silently. When finished reading, each person is to think of a question to ask about the paragraph. You then take turns asking your questions. Of course, students and teacher can look back to answer a question if they need to. Continue reading and taking turns asking questions for two or three more paragraphs. Then finish reading in the usual manner.

Your aim in this strategy is to model question-asking so that your students will do this on their own as they read. As they become familiar with the strategy, they can practice with each other as well as with you. Sometimes the questions you and your students create can be written down and used as a kind of quiz. If you are interested in learning more about reciprocal questioning, see the Manzo article listed in the bibliography.

▪ **Free Response** Another way to get your students actively involved while reading is to have them jot down what they are thinking as they read. Before they read a selection, ask them to mark certain places in the text where they will stop reading. Then have them read the selection. At the preselected stops, they should pause and write down ideas or questions they have. You can write down your own responses as you read the selection along with the students. When finished, share your thoughts with one another.

You can use these free responses as springboards for discussion. For example, you may note how the selection related to what your students already know and to their own lives. Or you may have students talk about information that surprised them or was new for them. You may also discuss the language of the selection, that is, words that vividly described events or sentences that seemed confusing to your students.

Integrating New Ideas

To help your students make connections between their reading, their experiences, and new ideas, you may want to try these two integration activities.

▪ **Theme Units** Since *Foundations* is already organized by units ("People," "Coping," "Messages," and "Cultures"), you can highlight these as themes by adding two simple activities.

Copyright © 1991 Scott, Foresman and Company.

Consider using *theme launchers,* such as books (fiction and nonfiction), poems, learner experiences, objects, or pictures to add information to the theme. These become an interesting way for learners to connect what they already know to new information they will encounter in the selections. For example, theme launchers for Unit 1, "People," might include newspaper clippings about current political figures, biographical sketches of famous people, or a family photo album. Those for the unit "Coping" may involve informational brochures on health issues, recipes for special diets, or a calorie chart. Consider keeping theme launchers in a box or a scrapbook to add to or review occasionally.

Graphic organizers can also be used to show connections between different selections in a unit, making a theme more apparent. You can do this easily by expanding on the maps and charts that are included in many of the *Foundations* lessons.

For example, early in Unit 2 students map what they already know about coping. Expand the maps throughout the unit by having your students add new information and ideas after they read each selection. As their maps enlarge, have them look for categories of information and create labels for them. For instance, students may develop categories such as parenting, job-hunting, and staying healthy. Consider combining individual student maps into one large group map that illustrates further the ideas related to the theme of coping. Areas of special interest could become individual or small-group projects that you and your students explore beyond the book.

▪ **Learning Logs** Learning logs help your students monitor and direct their own learning. Explain to your students that they are to keep a log in which they record what they learn. Tell them not to worry about spelling or grammar. To guide their responses, they can ask themselves questions such as these: ▪ What did I learn today?   ▪ What puzzled or confused me?   ▪ What did I enjoy, dislike, or accomplish in class today?   ▪ What new words do I know?

Provide ten minutes after each instructional session for students to write in their logs. Collect the logs regularly. You can use the logs to see what needs to be reviewed or clarified. Write comments directly to students in the log entries. This starts a conversation about learning between you and the student. Logs can also become the basis for instruction and a way to link what students know to new information they are learning.

Consider some of these whole-language activities in your instruction. They not only develop reading and writing but also invite adult learners to use reading and writing as tools for learning.

Copyright © 1991 Scott, Foresman and Company.

Key to Pronunciation

Pronunciations for a few words appear in the *Foundations* books. The following key has been used. The syllable that bears the greatest emphasis when the word is spoken appears in capital letters.

The key shows how common word sounds are indicated by diacritical marks in *The World Book Dictionary* and in the Scott, Foresman dictionaries. The pronunciation key also shows examples of the *schwa,* or unaccented vowel sound. The schwa is represented by ə.

It is a good idea to explain to your students how to interpret these pronunciations when they come to them in the book.

Letter or Mark	As in	Respelling	Example	
a	hat, map	a	ALPHABET	AL fuh beht
ā	age, face	ay	ASIA	AY zhuh
ã	care, air	ai	BAREBACK	BAIR bak
ä	father, far	ah	ARMISTICE	AHR muh stihs
ch	child, much	ch	CHINA	CHY nuh
e	let, best	eh	ESSAY	EHS ay
ē	equal, see,	ee	LEAF	leef
	machine, city		MARINE	muh REEN
ėr	term, learn,			
	sir, work	ur	PEARL	purl
i	it, pin, hymn	ih	SYSTEM	SIHS tuhm
ī	ice, five	y	OHIO	oh HY oh
		eye	IRIS	EYE rihs
k	coat, look	k	CORN	kawrn
o	hot, rock	ah	OTTAWA	AHT uh wuh
ō	open, go, grow,	oh	RAINBOW	RAYN boh
	château		TABLEAU	TAB loh
ô	order, all	aw	ORCHID	AWR kihd
			ALLSPICE	AWL spys
oi	oil, voice	oy	COINAGE	KOY nihj
			POISON	POY zuhn
ou	house, out	ow	FOUNTAIN	FOWN tuhn
s	say, nice	s	SPICE	spys
sh	she, abolition	sh	MOTION	MOH shuhn
u	cup, butter,	uh	STUDY	STUHD ee
	flood		BLOOD	bluhd
ù	full, put, wood	u	FULBRIGHT	FUL bryt
			WOOL	wul
ü	rule, move, food	oo	ZULU	ZOO loo
zh	pleasure	zh	ASIA	AY zhuh
ə	about, ameba	uh	BURMA	BUR muh
	taken, purple	uh	FIDDLE	FIHD uhl
	pencil	uh	CITIZEN	SIHT uh zuhn
	lemon	uh	LION	LY uhn
	circus	uh	CYPRUS	SY pruhs
	labyrinth	uh	PHYSIQUE	fuh ZEEK
	curtain	uh	MOUNTAIN	MOWN tuhn
	Egyptian	uh	GEORGIA	JAWR juh
	section	uh	LEGION	LEE juhn
	fabulous	uh	ANONYMOUS	uh NAHN uh muhs

From *The World Book Encyclopedia.* © 1989 World Book, Inc. Used with permission.

Copyright © 1991 Scott, Foresman and Company.

Bibliography

Altwerger, Bess; Edelsky, Carole; and Flores, Barbara M. "Whole Language: What's New." *The Reading Teacher* 40 (November 1987): 144–154.

Bacon, M. "What Adult Literacy Teachers Need to Know About Strategies for Focusing on Comprehension." *Lifelong Learning: The Adult Years,* vol. 6, no. 6 (1983): 4–5.

Barasovska, Joan. *Getting Started with Experience Stories.* Syracuse, NY: New Readers Press, 1988.

Bowren, Faye R., and Zintz, Miles V. *Teaching Reading in Adult Basic Education.* Dubuque, IA: William C. Brown, 1977.

Carpenter, Tracy. *The Right to Read Tutor's Handbook for the SCIL (Student Centered Individualized Learning) Program.* Toronto: Frontier College, 1986.

Colvin, Ruth J., and Root, Jane H. *TUTOR: Techniques Used in the Teaching of Reading,* 6th ed. Syracuse, NY: Literacy Volunteers of America, 1987.

Cross, Kathryn Patricia. *Adults as Learners: Increasing Participation and Facilitating Learning.* San Francisco: Jossey-Bass, 1981.

Davidson, Jane L., and Wheat, Thomas E. "Successful Literacy Experiences for Adult Illiterates." *Journal of Reading* 32 (January 1989): 342–346.

Duffy, Gerald G., et al. "Modeling Mental Processes Helps Poor Readers Become Strategic Readers." *The Reading Teacher* 41 (April 1988): 762–767.

Fingeret, Arlene. *Adult Literacy: Current and Future Directions.* ERIC Clearinghouse on Adult, Career, and Vocational Education. The National Center on Research in Education, Ohio State University, 1984 (ERIC Document Reproduction Service No. ED 246 308).

Flood, James, ed. *Promoting Reading Comprehension.* Newark, DE: International Reading Association, 1984.

Forester, Anne D. "Learning to Read and Write at 26." *Journal of Reading* 31 (April 1988): 604–613.

Fountas, Irene C., and Hannigan, Irene L. "Making Sense of Whole Language: The Pursuit of Informed Teaching." *Childhood Education,* Spring 1989, pp. 133–137.

Freire, Paulo. *Pedagogy of the Oppressed.* New York: Herder and Herder, 1970.

Goodman, Kenneth. *What's Whole in Whole Language?* Portsmouth, NH: Heinemann, 1986.

Hatch, Evelyn. "Reading a Second Language." In *Teaching English as a Second or Foreign Language.* New York: Newbury House Publishers, 1979.

Heathington, B. S. "Expanding the Definition of Literacy for Adult Remedial Readers." *Journal of Reading* 31 (December 1987): 213–217.

Heilman, Arthur. *Phonics in Proper Perspective.* Columbus, OH: Charles E. Merrill, 1985.

Hermann, Beth Ann. "Two Approaches for Helping Poor Readers Become More Strategic." *The Reading Teacher* 42 (October 1988): 24–28.

Johnson, Dale D., and Pearson, P. David. *Teaching Reading Vocabulary.* New York: Holt, Rinehart and Winston, 1984.

Jones, Edward V. *Reading Instruction for the Adult Illiterate.* Chicago: American Library Association, 1981.

Kazemek, Francis E., and Rigg, Pat. "Four Poets: Modern Poetry in the Adult Literacy Classroom." *Journal of Reading* 30 (December 1986): 218–225.

Knowles, Malcolm. *The Modern Practice of Adult Education: From Pedagogy to Androgogy,* 2nd ed. New York: Cambridge Book Co., 1980.

Knox, Alan B. *Adult Development and Learning.* San Francisco: Jossey-Bass, 1977.

Lane, Martha A., ed. *Handbook for Volunteer Reading Aides.* Philadelphia: Lutheran Church Women, 1984.

Copyright © 1991 Scott, Foresman and Company.

Manzo, A. V. "The Request Procedure." *Journal of Reading* 11 (1969): 123–126.

Mayes, Cheryl. "Five Critical Thinking Strategies for Adult Basic Education Learners." *Lifelong Learning* 10 (May 1987): 11–13, 25.

McNeil, John D. *Reading Comprehension: New Directions for Classroom Practice.* 2nd ed. Glenview, IL: Scott, Foresman and Company, 1987.

Meyer, Valerie, and Keefe, Donald. *Reading for Meaning: Selected Teaching Strategies.* Glenview, IL: Scott, Foresman and Company, 1990.

Mocker, Donald W., ed. *Teaching Reading to Adults.* Scott, Foresman/AAACE Adult Educator Series. Glenview, IL: Scott, Foresman and Company, 1986.

Norman, C., and Malicky, G. "Stages in the Reading Development of Adults." *Journal of Reading* 30 (January 1987): 302–307.

Ottoson, Gerald, et al. *Tutoring Small Groups: Basic Reading.* Syracuse, NY: Literacy Volunteers of America, 1985.

Padak, Gary M., and Padak, Nancy D. "Guidelines and a Holistic Method for Adult Basic Reading Programs." *Journal of Reading* 30 (March 1987): 490–496.

Palmieri, Mary Ann De Vita. "Julie: A Special Kind of Illiteracy." *Lifelong Learning* 12 (October 1988): 7–9.

Pearson, P. David. "Changing the Face of Reading Comprehension." *The Reading Teacher* 38 (April 1985): 724–738.

Perin, Dolores. "Schema Activation, Cooperation and Adult Literacy Instruction." *Journal of Reading* 32 (October 1988): 54–62.

Pinell, Gay Su, and Matlin, Myrna. *Teachers and Research: Language Learning in the Classroom.* Newark, DE: International Reading Association, 1989.

Raphael, Taffy E. "Teaching Question Answer Relationships, Revisited." *The Reading Teacher* 39 (February 1986): 516–522.

Rauch, Sidney J., and Sanacore, J., eds. *Handbook for the Volunteer Tutor.* 2nd ed. Newark, DE: International Reading Association, 1985.

Rice, Gail. *Preparing Your Own ABE Adult Basic Education Reading Materials.* Lifelong Learning Books Teacher Resource Series. Glenview, IL: Scott, Foresman and Company, 1990.

Rigg, Pat, and Kazemek, Francis. "For Adults Only: Reading Materials for Adult Literacy Students." *Journal of Reading* 28 (May 1985): 728–731.

Rosenthal, Nadine. *Teach Someone to READ: A Step-by-Step Guide for Literacy Tutors.* Belmont, CA: Fearon/David S. Lake Publishers, 1987.

Scales, Alice, and Burley, Jo Anne. "A Holistic Approach to Teaching Adult Literacy Techniques." *Lifelong Learning* 12 (November 1988): 26–28.

Shuman, R. Baird. "Some Assumptions About Adult Reading Instruction." *Journal of Reading* 32 (January 1989): 348–354.

Smith, Frank. *Reading Without Nonsense.* 2nd ed. New York: Teacher's College Press, 1985.

Tierney, Robert J.; Readence, John E.; and Dishner, Ernest K. *Reading Strategies and Practices, A Compendium,* 2nd ed. Newton, MA: Allyn and Bacon, 1985.

Weaver, Constance. *Reading Process and Practice: From Socio-Psycholinguistics to Whole Language.* Portsmouth, NH: Heinemann, 1988.

Copyright © 1991 Scott, Foresman and Company.